THE MEANING OF SARKOZY

THE MEANING OF SARKOZY

ALAIN BADIOU

Translated by David Fernbach

VERSO

London • New York

This edition first published by Verso 2008
© Verso 2008
Translation @ David Fernbach 2008
First published as *De quoi Sarkozy est-il le nom?*
© Nouvelles Éditions Lignes, 2007

1 3 5 7 9 10 8 6 4 2

Verso
UK: 6 Meard Street, London W1F 0EG
USA: 20 Jay Street, Suite 1010, Brooklyn, NY 11201
www.versobooks.com

Verso is the imprint of New Left Books

ISBN-13: 978-1-84467-309-4

British Library Cataloguing in Publication Data
A catalogue record for this book is available from the British Library

Library of Congress Cataloging-in-Publication Data
A catalog record for this book is available from the Library of Congress

Typeset by Hewer Text UK Ltd, Edinburgh
Printed in the USA by Maple Vail

Contents

Introduction to the English-Language Edition

Many of my friends abroad still have an image of France drawn from the most glorious episodes of our political and intellectual history: the great thinkers of the eighteenth-century Enlightenment, the Revolution of 1792–94, the nineteenth-century insurrections of the workers and common people, the July days of 1830 and the Commune of 1871; I could also mention June 1848, the formation of the Popular Front in 1936 and the great contribution made to the International Brigades in Spain, the Resistance, the social legislation of the Liberation, the great philosophical and progressive movement from the 1950s to the '70s, May 1968 and its consequences . . . The result of all this is that when a fact of similar kind (political, intellectual, or both) but with an unquestionably reactionary character happens in France, these friends are amazed and wonder what is going on. Each time I have to remind them that France is also a deeply conservative country, which responds to the revolutionary episodes in its history with long sequences of black reaction, and that those who have come to power in these painful sequences have never lacked the support of numerous and well-established intellectual cliques. There is a second history of France, longer and more bound up with the structures of state than the insurrectionary history written by the broad masses. We can think of the Thermidoreans after 1794, shielding if not actually practising a white terror that claimed a far greater number of victims than the Terror of the great Jacobins; or the Restoration after 1815, with the 'milliard' in compensation paid to the émigrés and the revenge of the privileged of all kinds; the swindle that brought the Orleanist monarchy to power in 1830 with the slogan 'enrich yourselves' that became the national hymn; the interminable reign of Napoleon III and his bankers, which followed from the revolution of February 1848 and the massacre of the Paris workers in June the same year; the consensus around horrendous colonial expeditions, in particular the conquest of Algeria; the repression of the Commune by the Versaillais and their frenetic massacre; the nationalist butchery of 1914–18; right after the Popular Front we had Pétain, after the red years of 1966–76 we had Giscard d'Estaing. And each time, a whole court of service intellectuals praising the re-establishment of order and grizzling over the 'horrors' of the revolutionaries. Eulogists of the restored monarchy under Louis XVIII, lickspittles of the Second Empire, Versaillais pen-pushers drunk on the corpses of workers, high-spirited youngsters of the anti-Bolshevik legions, Pétainists and collaborators . . .

It should be no surprise, then, that in the wake of May 1968 and its consequences a band of impostors took the stage under the bizarre signboard of 'new philosophy', charged with presenting, yet again, the abominations of the revolutionaries, extolling capitalism, parliamentary 'democracy', the US Army and the West. This was just a continuation of the great invariants of our history: outbreaks of impressive popular hysteria, to be sure, but also rancid reactionary obsessions.

I try to show here how the election of Sarkozy is a concentrate of this second history of France, the history of dark and ruthless conservatism. This is why I have called its principle one of 'transcendental Pétainism', giving it a name with a bit of a historical echo. I also try to show how, against this 'restoration in the restoration', it is necessary to go back to the most general and essential principles, what I call the 'communist hypothesis', of which I offer an interpretation divided into periods. These are long-term perspectives, triggered by an episode that one might believe is relatively unimportant.

Do I then have to despair of my fellow citizens? As we know, carried away by the fearful vertigo of their total political disorientation, the electorate chose a character from whom they soon saw nothing good could be expected. It might well be, then, that at the end of the day 'Sarkozy' will denote the end of this gloomy and increasingly sinister reaction that began in the 1980s and has not stopped laying waste to our country, its substance as well as its intelligence. Let's hope so.

My enemies – and there are a good number of these – afraid as they are that the hope will return that a different world is possible than the one that they serve, have insinuated that I am anti-Semitic: a trick they invented two or three years ago and use against anyone who displeases them. I am proud to be attacked by true professionals of this insinuation.[1] Clearly, when I criticize the policy of the state

---

1 [Accusations of anti-Semitism on Badiou's part were made after the publication of the texts in *Circonstances 3* (Paris: Lignes Manifeste, 2005) (in English they are collected together in *Polemics* (London: Verso, 2006). One of the most egregious examples of this claim was made by Eric Marty in his book *Une querelle avec Alain Badiou, philosophe* (Paris: Editions Gallimard, 2007).]

of Israel, which is the least of things, or when I show how some of them, ignominiously perched on the piles of dead of the Extermination, attempt to stick the name 'Jew' on the fate of the West and its master, the United States, thus stripping this word of its great revolutionary tradition and prostituting it in a way that is not only detestable but actually dangerous for those who claim it, I give these professionals grist for their mill. I repeat here, however, for those of these professionals whose language is English, that if I cross the path of one of them, being as I am a champion of direct action rather than legal process, they will receive the slap due to a stupid slanderer.

As far as the present book goes, you'd be hard-pressed to find anything on which to pin the infamous charge of anti-Semitism. Not a mention of 'Jews', not so much as a passing allusion? No problem! It takes more than a little difficulty like this to deter those sycophantic professional informers who'll always find something to pounce on (even if they have to lie through their teeth). A certain character of admittedly limited intelligence, Monsieur Assouline, remarked on his blog – you're either modern or you're not – that I called those Socialists who joined the Sarkozy government 'rats' and christened Sarkozy himself the 'Rat Man'. Anyone with even a modicum of education would immediately have grasped that I am referring here (not without a rhetorical subtlety they should surely commend) to the metaphor of rats leaving a sinking ship, to the legend of the Pied Piper who led the rats out of the city, and to Freud's celebrated case of the Rat Man.[2] Does Monsieur Assouline have any education? He knows well enough, at least, where he wants

2 [Pierre Assouline is a writer and journalist who runs a popular blog called *La République des Livres*.]

to end up. Since the last war and the Nazis, he proclaims (follow closely), no one has ever treated anyone at all as a rat. On the other hand, Sarkozy has certain Jewish ancestors. And so . . . You see? OK? You really do see?

The oddest thing is that the leader of these media intellectuals committed to Restoration, Bernard-Henri Lévy, should jump on the bandwagon without even citing his inglorious source. Thus we read in *Le Monde*:

> In a recent book, *The Meaning of Sarkozy* [*De quoi Sarkozy est-il le nom?*], Alain Badiou used his just struggle against what he finds 'disgusting' to reintroduce into the political lexicon those zoological metaphors ('rats', 'the Rat Man') that Sartre unequivocally showed, in his preface to [Fanon's] *The Wretched of the Earth*, always bear the mark of fascism.[3]

There we are! Pierre Vidal-Naquet, a man greatly missed, already showed, with his immense knowledge, how Bernard-Henri Lévy was also a professional of howlers and ignorance. And Sartre, throughout his essential essay *The Communists and Peace*, written in 1953–54, referred to anti-Communists as 'rats'. He certainly did so with far more good humour than the way he himself was treated as a 'typing hyena', not by the fascists but by his Communist allies. The same Sartre uttered the famous sentence that 'every anti-Communist is a swine'. So we see that, well after the war, animals were still used on all sides . . . I particularly like the Chinese usage to denote two apparent enemies who are really complicit with one another – as for Mao were

3 'De quoi Siné est-il le nom?', Bernard-Henri Lévy, *Le Monde*, 21 July 2008.

the Soviet Union under Khrushchev and the United States under Kennedy, and I could say the same for my part of the Socialist Party and Sarkozy in matters of xenophobic and 'security' legislation. The Chinese then spoke of 'two badgers from the same hill'. I love this image, and used it in the present book with reference to a fact that my English readers will appreciate: during the election campaign, both Sarkozy and Ségolène Royal praised Tony Blair – Blair, *blaireau* [badger] . . . translate it how you can! So I've added to 'zoological metaphors' the ignominy of a play on words.

I can only plead guilty and expose myself to Sarkozy's legislation on recidivism (legislation, let us say in passing, that is openly directed against ordinary people, and therefore abominable). I claim the right to use 'zoological metaphors' – I don't have a hang-up about them. It is characteristic of politics that there are enemies, even if capitalo-parliamentarism presses its domination to the point of trying to make us forget this. And why the hell, if there are real enemies, shouldn't I be allowed to insult them? To compare them with vultures, jackals, reptiles, even rats – not to mention hyenas, whether typing or otherwise? Not everyone can be compared with an eagle, like Bossuet, or a bull, like the Fourth Republic Prime Minister Joseph Laniel, even a fox, as Mitterrand regularly was. And now, ladies and gentlemen, a touch of humour. If Sélogène Royal makes me think of a painted goat, and Prime Minister Fillon a sleeping weasel, there's no need to hit the roof.

Enjoy your reading, whatever your favourite animal.

Paris,
22 July 2008

1 Before the Election

We are now in the midst of an election campaign to appoint the president. How can I avoid speaking of it?[1] A tricky one that . . . Philosophy may resist the content of opinions, but that does not mean it can ignore their existence, especially when this becomes literally frenetic, as it has done in recent weeks.

I discussed voting in *Circonstances 1*, with regard to the presidential election of 2002.[2] I emphasized on that occasion that little credence should be placed in such an irrational procedure, and analysed in terms of this concrete example the disastrous consequences of that parliamentary fetishism which in our society fills the place of 'democracy'. The role of collective affects could not, I said, be underestimated in this kind of circumstance, organized from one end to the other by the state, and relayed by its series of apparatuses – precisely those that Louis Althusser aptly named the

1 This section more or less repeats the session of my monthly seminar at the École Normale Supérieure, in the context of the activities of the Centre Internationale d'Étude de la Philosophie Française Contemporaine (CIEPFC), held on 4 April 2007.
2 See Alain Badiou, *Polemics* (London: Verso, 2006).

'ideological state apparatuses': parties, of course, but also the civil service, trade unions, media of all kinds. These latter institutions, notably of course television, but more subtly the written press, are quite spectacular powers of unreason and ignorance. Their particular function is to spread the dominant affects. They played a good part in the 'Le Pen psychosis' of 2002, which, after the old Pétainist – a knackered old horse from a ruined stable – had passed the first round, threw masses of terrified young *lycéens* and right-minded intellectuals into the arms of Chirac, who, no longer himself in his heyday as far as political vigour was concerned, did not expect so much. With the cavalcade headed by Sarkozy, and the Socialist Party choosing as candidate a hazy *bourgeoise* whose thinking, if it exists, is somewhat concealed, we reap the fatal consequence of this madness five years down the road.

This time round, the collective emotion that propels a kind of twitchy accountant into the limelight, mayor of a town where hereditary wealth is concentrated, and moreover visibly uncultured, could be called, as it was at the time of the French Revolution, *la grande peur*.

The elections to which the state summons us are in fact dominated by the contradictory entanglement of two kinds of fear.

There is first of all the fear I shall call essential, which marks the subjective situation of dominant and privileged people who sense that their privileges are conditional and under threat and that their domination is perhaps only provisional and already shaky. In France, a middle-sized power for which one cannot foresee any glorious future – unless it invents a politics that would reverse the country's insignificance and make it an emancipatory reference point for the planet – the negative affect is particularly violent and wretched. It translates into fear of foreigners, of workers, of the people, of youngsters from the *banlieues*, Muslims, black Africans . . . This fear, conservative and gloomy, creates the desire for a master who will protect you, even if only while oppressing and impoverishing you all the more. We are familiar today with the features of this master: Sarko, a jittery cop who sets the whole place on fire, and for whom media coups, friendly financiers and backstage graft make up the whole secret of politics. With this very miniature Napoleon, and faced with the internal perils made real by fear, the state ends up taking the one-sided form that Genet previously gave it in his play *The Balcony*, that of the police chief whose dream costume is a gigantic rubber penis. It is no paradox, then, if Sarkozy, a minuscule character in direct communication with the lowest form of opinion polls, hoisted himself up to the profound thought that paedophilia is a genetic defect, and he himself a born heterosexual.[3] What better symbol of the unconscious fears whose mustiness is conveyed by the political spectacle than this paedophilia, which as we have seen for years, culminating with the Outreau trial, symbolizes, in our genuinely pornographic society, the buried desires that are not allowed to exist? And what worthier master to put an end to this accursed and abstract paedophilia, and at the same stroke to deal with all these foreigners and foreign ways, than a reinforced-concrete heterosexual? Celebrity politics is not my cup of tea, but I would place some hope here in the candidate's strange wife, this Cécilia who may

3 [See the dialogue between Sarkozy and Michel Onfray in *Philosophie Magazine*, no. 8, 2007, available online at: <http://www.philomag.com/article,dialogue,nicolas-sarkozy-et-michel-onfray-confidences-entre-ennemis,288.php>.]

actually throw some unexpected light on her husband's genetic claims.

Opposed to this primitive fear, in electoral terms, is not, as it should be, a clear assertion that is different in principle from the variations on the policing theme. It is on the contrary another fear: the fear that the first fear provokes, by conjuring up a type of master, the jumpy cop, with whom the Socialist petty bourgeois is unfamiliar and doesn't like. This is a second fear, a derivative fear, the content of which, we have to say, is indiscernible beyond the affect involved. At the level of their broad mass support, neither side, not the UMP rank-and-file nor the Socialist activists, have the least positive vision to counter the massive effect of unleashed capitalism. Neither asserts, against the external and internal division globalized capitalism provokes, that there is only one world. In particular, no alliance with the persecuted, with the inhabitants of the 'other' world, is proposed by the Socialist Party. It simply envisages harvesting the dubious benefits of the fear of fear.

For both electoral camps, indeed, the world does not exist. On such questions as Palestine, Iran, Afghanistan (where French troops are engaged), Lebanon (likewise), Africa (swarming with French military personnel), there is a total consensus, and no one envisages opening the least public discussion on these questions of war and peace. Nor is there any serious questioning of the villainous laws voted day after day against undocumented workers, youngsters from the poor districts and the incurably ill. Since fear is set against fear, the implication is that the only questions that really move people are of this kind: Should we be more afraid of the Tamil street-sweeper or of the cop harassing him? Or is global warming more or less of a peril than the arrival of Malian cooks? This is the way of the electoral circus.

The subjective index of this omnipresent affective negativity is the cleavage of the electoral subject. Everything in fact leads us to expect a massive vote, to the point that even their own friends seek to intimidate those who, like me, have the firm intention not to take part in this crooked summons from the state. The vote thus operates almost like a form of superego. The polls, however, indicate massive indecision right up to the last minute. In other words, this probably massive vote, which people even experience as compulsory, carries no conviction beyond the affects involved. One may well believe that to decide between fear, and fear of fear, is a delicate undertaking.

Let us assume that politics is what I think it is, which can be summed up in the following definition: organized collective action, following certain principles, and aiming to develop in reality the consequences of a new possibility repressed by the dominant state of affairs. Then we have to conclude that the vote to which we are summoned is an essentially apolitical practice. It is subject in fact to the non-principle of affect. Hence the cleavage between a formal imperative and an unconquerable hesitancy about any possible affirmative convictions. It is good to vote, to give form to my fears, but it is hard to believe that *what I vote for* is right. What is lacking in the vote is nothing less than the *real*.

Concerning the real, it will be said that the second fear, which we can call opposition, is still further removed from this than the original fear, which we can call reaction. For people react, if in a terrorized, incriminating or even criminal fashion, to some effective situation. Whereas the opposition simply fears the amplitude of this reaction, and is thus one notch further from anything that effectively exists.

These elections are a confused crystallization of the fact that the negativity of the Left, or of opposition, has the notable weakness of being in a confused sharing of the real along with what it opposes. For the real by which this Left sustains itself, at a great distance, is simply that which creates the original fear, that fear whose dreaded effects are the whole content of the opposition.

Too devoid of the real, or sharing in the reality of its supposed adversary, the second or Socialist fear can only fix its sights on the vague, the uncertain, a haziness of language with no mooring in the world. This is Ségolène Royal. She is the imaginary propensity in which the lack of anything real is articulated, the second fear as empty exaltation. She is nothingness as the subjective pole of the fears organized by the election ritual.

I shall propose a theorem: every chain of fears leads to nothingness, and voting is the operation of this. If this is not a political operation, as I maintain, what is its nature? Well, voting is a state operation. And it is only by assuming that politics and the state are identical that voting can be conceived as a political procedure.[4]

I spoke just now of the electoral cleavage: voting is on a mass scale and experienced as an imperative, whereas political or ideological conviction is floating or even nonexistent. This cleavage is interesting and positive to the extent that

4 For three decades, Sylvain Lazarus has drawn the consequences of his most powerful axiom: that a politics of emancipation (which he calls, for technical reasons, 'politics in interiority') can only be conceived on the basis of a clearly made separation between politics and the state. This amounts, in the political process itself, to organizing, thinking and acting at a remove from the state. His major work, *Anthropologie du nom* (Paris: Editions du Seuil, 1996), has to be read.

it unconsciously signifies the distance between politics and state. In the case that we are concerned with here, for want of any genuine politics, there is an incorporation of fear into the state, as the substratum of its own independence. Fear serves to validate the state. The electoral operation incorporates fear, and the fear of fear, into the state, with the result that a mass subjective element comes to validate the state. We can say that, after this election, the winner – very likely Sarkozy – will have become the legitimate head of state by feathering his nest with fear. He will then have his hands free, because once the state has been occupied by fear, it can freely create fear.

The final dialectic is that of fear and terror. A state legitimized by fear is virtually fit to become terroristic.

Is there a contemporary terrorism, a democratic terror? This is quite rampant at the present time. Democratic forms are being found for a state terror at the level of contemporary technology: radar, photos, Internet controls, systematic bugging of all telephones, mapping of people's movements . . . The perspective of the state that we face is one of virtual terror, its key mechanism being surveillance, and increasingly also informing.

Should we speak, like our Deleuzian friends, of a 'society of control' essentially different from a 'society of sovereignty'? I do not think so. Control will change into pure and simple state terrorism as soon as circumstances turn at all serious. Already, suspects are sent to be tortured by less considerate 'friends'. We shall end up doing this at home. Fear never has any other future than terror, in the most ordinarily established sense.

I shall make a digression here. Philosophers know better than others, when they really do their work, that the world of men and women, individuals and societies, is always less novel than the inhabitants of this world imagine. And technology, which is presented as the ultimate meaning and novelty of our future, whether glorious or catastrophic, almost always remains in the service of the most antique procedures. From this point of view, the convinced 'modern' who sees progress everywhere that capitalism deploys its machinery, and the semi-religious ecologist who clings, against productive artifice, to the fantasy of a benign nature, share an identical stupidity.

To return to our fears. What is the reason for this fearful tension that promises us an excruciating series of turns of the screw on the part of the state? It is that the truth of the situation is war. Bush, whose words it would be prudent to take literally rather than mock, envisioned 'very long war' against terrorism. And, indeed, the West is increasingly engaged on a number of fronts. The mere preservation of the existing order is warfare, as this order is pathological. The gigantic disparity, the duality of rich and poor worlds, is maintained by force. War is the global perspective of democracy. Our governments try to make people believe that war is elsewhere, and that war is waged for their protection. But this war has no fixed location, it cannot be readily contained in space. The West wants to prevent the appearance, anywhere, of what it really fears: a pole of power heterogeneous to its domination, a 'rogue state' as Bush puts it, which would have the means to measure up to the triumphant 'democracies' of today, without in any way sharing their vision of the world, and would not be prepared to sit down with them to share the delights of the world market and electoral numbers. The West will not prevail, it can only delay this event by increasingly savage external war and internal terrorism. For there are rogues at home, too, alas! Those whom a Socialist minister called 'little savages',[5] and whom Sarkozy treats as 'scum' [*racaille*]. A future alliance between rogue states abroad and rogues at home – that's really something to fear! We have here the possible political profile for the creation of a *grande peur*.

The key point is that there is a dialectic of fear and war. We make war abroad, our governments say, to protect ourselves from war at home. We go and hunt out terrorists in Afghanistan or Chechnya who would otherwise arrive en masse in our own countries and organize here the 'scum' and the 'little savages'. And, in this way, they create fully formed, among the people of the privileged countries, the fear of war, internal and external, since war is at the same time there (far away) and not there (in our midst), in a problematic liaison of the local and the global.

What must be borne in mind is that this question has a particular history in France. The typical name of this alliance between war and fear, in our country, is 'Pétainism'. The mass idea of Pétainism, what made for its momentary but very widespread success between 1940 and 1944, was that, after the trials of the 'phoney war', Pétain would protect the French people from the most disastrous effects of the world war – permit them to remain at a distance. The fear generated in 1914–18 created the fear necessary for Pétainism in 1940. It was Pétain who said that we should be more afraid of war than of defeat. It is better to live, or at least survive, than to make trouble. The French overwhelmingly accepted

5 [Reference to Jean-Pierre Chevènement, then minister of the interior in the Jospin government, who referred in a notorious statement in January 1999 on television to young criminals as 'sauvageons'.]

the relative tranquillity that came with the acceptance of defeat.

And we should not hide the fact that this Pétainism was partly successful: the French came through the war very quietly compared with the Russians or even the British. This is a point I shall return to later. Let us simply say here that the analogous 'Pétainism' of today consists in maintaining that the French simply have to accept the laws of the world – the Yankee model, servility towards the powerful, the domination of the rich, hard work by the poor, the surveillance of everyone, systematic suspicion of foreigners living here, contempt for people who do not live like we do – and then all will be well. Sarkozy's programme, like that of Pétain himself, is work, family and country. Work: if you want to earn a few bob, do as much overtime as you like. Family: abolition of inheritance tax, perpetuation of hereditary wealth. Country: although the only thing that distinguishes it today is this wretched fear, France is tremendous, we should be proud of being French. In any case, 'the French' (Sarkozy?) are certainly superior to 'the Africans' (who?).

Unfortunately, these maxims are scarcely any different from the sentimental preaching of Ségolène Royal.

Beyond the electoral ups and downs, the imperative need is to do everything possible to prevent an analogous Pétainism becoming the general logic of the situation. With Sarkozy, but also with his rival, there is the possibility of a neo-Pétainism on a mass scale. Pétainism, rather than fascism, which is an affirmative force. Pétainism presents the subjective abominations of fascism (fear, informing, contempt for others) without its vital spirit. To eliminate this peril, we have to do as much as we can to develop the alliance of the fearless.

Mao said of war: 'We do not like war. But we are not

afraid of it.' Courage is certainly the number-one virtue today. The courage to withdraw both from the original fear and from the fear of fear. Mao also said: 'Reject your illusions and prepare for struggle.' What is the most pervasive illusion today? It is the illusion cultivated by the Left in general, and Ségolène Royal in particular: that we can trust fear (i.e. the fear of fear) to avoid the reactive effects of fear, the fidgety cop as the man in charge. But no! That way we'll get both fear and the cop as well!

Rejecting illusions always means reorientation. It means affirming that an orientation of thought and existence can be asserted beyond affects. Voting in general, and in particular the vote proposed to us today, is a state mechanism that presents disorientation itself as a choice. It's a different interpretation of the cleavage that I spoke of above: disoriented minds, who don't know what saint or what Pétain to appeal to, are convinced all the same of the great importance of voting. So they go and vote for one or other of the indistinguishable candidates. They are in fact completely disoriented, as is shown when they change their mind next time round, just to see. And yet the state and the unanimous voice of the press, in their commentaries on the vote, present this evident disorientation as a choice, thus disclaiming any responsibility. The government, which would not be very different if it were chosen by lottery, declares that it has been mandated by the choice of the citizens and can act in the name of this choice. Voting thus produces a singular illusion, which passes this disorientation through the fallacious filter of a choice.

'The French have decided . . .' says the right-minded press. They have not decided anything at all, and moreover, this collective – 'the French' – lacks any existence. Why on

earth should 51 per cent of French people be 'the French'?
Is it not a constant of history that 'the French' has often
meant a small minority, as for example at the key moment
of the German occupation, when it meant the very small
minority represented by the resistance, and for at least two
years hardly anyone at all? The rest were broadly Pétainist,
which meant, in the conditions of the time, that they were
in no way 'French', but fearful servants of Nazi Germany.
This is a very characteristic French trait: when the question
of the country's existence is really at stake, what constitutes
France, against a dense reactionary and fearful background,
is a minority that is active and admirable, but numerically
very weak. Our country has only existed and will only exist,
in whatever form it takes, by the acts of those who have
not accepted the abasements that the logic of the survival
of privileges, or just 'realistic' conformity with the laws of
the world, universally require. These are the people who
have chosen, and they certainly did not do so by voting.

'Reject our illusions' means categorically denying that
voting is the operation of a genuine choice. It means iden-
tifying it as an organized disorientation, which gives the
state personnel a free hand. The whole problem then is to
affirmatively reject this illusion, and to find elsewhere the
principle of an orientation of thought and existence. To
arrive at this, to identify the illusion as an illusion and reject
it – which means, among other things, not expecting
anything from the vote – we must, to recapitulate our
analysis, bring together five terms:

1. The reality of a world: the situation, and what we should
call it. Today I would say that it is war, both external (military
interventions) and internal (war against the people, the poor

and/or those of foreign origin, under cover of the 'anti-terrorist struggle'), that is the reality of the contemporary world.

2. The suitable maxim for a general orientation in this situation. The principle that, bearing on an existence as does any true principle, separates itself from domination and opens the field of the possible, is simply: there is only one world. We shall demonstrate this later on.

3. The structure of the illusion and its future. The illusion is not to see that it is the state that constructs the fallacious appearance of a political choice on the basis of the malleable material formed by public disorientation. Voting is just the operation of this appearance, which today only configures affects of fear. In short, voting is the fictitious figure of a choice, imposed on an essential disorientation.

4. Orientation. The place for this is at a remove from the state, thus outside of voting. Its role is to construct something unprecedented in the real. It consists in incorporating oneself into a certain truth process, in particular alongside the direct political organization of those who, even here, are kept outside of the (false) single world, relegated to the 'other' world. At the heart of this exiled world proletariat are the workers of foreign origin. And at the heart of this heart, those without papers.

5. Becoming-subject is the result of incorporation conceived as orientation. Human individuals, trained as animals who only know their immediate interests in the marketplace, make themselves one component among others in the body of truth, and by doing so go beyond themselves as a subject. Since we are in a landscape of war, and our specific local illusion is Pétainism (i.e. to remain sheltered from global earthquakes, whatever the price to pay: Jews

handed over to be massacred, Africans handed over to the police, children chased out of schools . . .), then to say 'there is only one world' means emerging from our shelter to make this maxim effective.

How can we recognize those who overcome their supposed 'free individuality', i.e. who overcome the stereotype in which they are dissolved (and what could be more monotonous, more uniform, than the 'free' individuals of commodity society, the civilized petty bourgeois repeating their laughable obsessions like well-fed parrots?) and attain the local steadfastness of a trans-individual truth? Their becoming-subject is attested, for example, in the conviction that to hold a meeting able to reach a conclusion and establish a duration sheltered from the schedules of the state, with four African workers from a hostel, a student, a Chinese textile worker, a postman, two housewives and a few stragglers from a housing estate, is infinitely more important, in an infinity itself incommensurable, than to drop the name of an indiscernible politician into the state counting-box.

2 After the Election

Have we not gathered here this evening, like everyone else, to discuss the consecration of our new president?[1] If I consider those inspired by a minimum of genuine thought, a conviction, a few fragments of historical knowledge, I seem to discover in them, after Sarkozy's untroubled victory, a somewhat depressive subjectivity. By your mere presence here, I credit you with belonging to the category to which I refer, that of people who are distressed by the disorientation organized by capital and its servants, rather than gratified by it. And I sense that, no matter how pressing my propaganda of maintaining a stoic indifference beneath the hail of votes, you seem to have received a blow. An expected blow, to be sure, but still violent enough.

I would like to start by analysing the feeling that disturbs you, which is that something unfortunate has happened, something that you don't like in the least.

Between you and me, for people with experience such as ourselves it is not just because a president has been

1 This section takes up material from my seminar held on 16 May 2007.

elected that something has happened. I have said enough about voting for you to know that, if something has indeed happened, we shall not find out what it is in the register of mere electoral succession. Which leads me to a preliminary meditation on what it is to feel struck by a blow, with the resulting experience of being a little blind, somewhat uncertain, and finally a bit depressed. Yes, dear friends, I detect in this hall the odour of depression. I assume, however, that it has taken more than just Sarkozy to depress you! What depresses you, therefore, is what Sarkozy is the name of. This is what should be borne in mind: you feel the advent of what Sarkozy is the name of as a blow struck by something, the no doubt disgusting something of which little Sarkozy is the servant.

It is often said that the most terrible blows are unexpected blows, accidents, mysterious suicides . . . But there is also something particularly nasty about expected blows. You know how sometimes one says, 'If I do this, then this other person will surely do that,' and it is often very unpleasant to see that they do indeed do that. It would be better if they disappointed our prediction, and their action was for once unexpected. But no! This vote, which has done no more than name the coming to pass of the disgusting thing, has the complete structure of an expected blow. Contrary to what often happens, it is the candidate who was ahead in the polls from the start of the official race who has won. Like a horse race in which the punters' favourite starts in front, remains in the lead for the whole course, and wins. It is not funny, it is even depressing. Anyone with a feeling for risk, for rupture, for wagers, for exceptions, would prefer it if an unknown nag were to win. But on this occasion, the nag lost, as she deserved.

And despite knowing what a nag she was, and that her convictions were both suspect and vague, we are all a little depressed just the same. Ask yourselves therefore what is the precise nature of this completely predictable blow you've suffered.

I offered on the last occasion an analysis of the electoral context, before the numerical decision, and said that the situation was one of a conflict between two fears, an original fear and a derivative one. The original fear belongs to that section of the population who dread something happening that will precipitate their decline. This original fear is focused on the traditional scapegoats – foreigners, the poor, distant countries that we do not want to resemble. It has for a long while been mustered and emblematized in the old discourse of Le Pen and the National Front, in the wretched style of the Pétainist revanchists. Then there is a second fear, the fear of the other fear, the fear of what this original fear will lead to. The conflict between the two has been sealed by the victory of the original fear, and after all this victory is not without a certain logic. If you have to be afraid, then it's better to be afraid of something other than simple fear. The original fear carried the day; that is the first component of the blow. This is readily visible in the faces of the mass of those rejoicing in this success: they think that the little excitable guy from Neuilly will build a Great Wall on the Chinese model to keep out the troublemakers, and that even if we can never be without fear, something impossible for any reactionary, we can at least be confident that the state will attend to our fears with a welcome vigilance. You can read on the mugs of the celebrating Sarkozy-ists a kind of impulsive excess in relation to this original fear, which they believe the new little president shares, making him close to themselves, while knowing how to limit its countless and perverse causes.

For my part, if I were afraid, I would in no way look to this kind of character to put me right, and for a very good reason: I am convinced that Sarkozy, who cannot go anywhere without being surrounded by a thick wall of body-guards, is not very dangerous. Like all who believe they can get by in all circumstances through the corruption of adversaries and a barrage of announcements, Sarkozy has a boundless dread of any real test. If I am right, what Sarkozy is most afraid of is that his own fear should become visible. Which, I might say in passing, brings him close to the Socialists, if it is true that the passion of the Socialist clientele is fear of fear. The two should get on together very well. This is a hypothesis, of course, but I would bet that it will not be long before we see the deleterious effects of Sarkozy's own fear. That is the first element in the rupture with Gaullism, even under the decayed and moribund form this had under Chirac. For the main political virtue of de Gaulle, perhaps his only one, was never to be afraid.

The element of impulse is certainly there, among all who imagine that with Sarkozy they have a brother-in-fear who is also an adept of the counter-fear. As for those who shared this fear of fear, here they are in the depression of this general negative impulse, which formed the background landscape and to which they have now been purely and simply returned.

The second element is that of nostalgia. An old world is crumbling. This old world is simply the one that arose from the Second World War, in the sense that Gaullists and Communists in France shared the same verdict on the war, on Pétainism, the Resistance and the Liberation. More generally, it is a whole orientation of parliamentary life that has been put out of joint, one that could unambiguously refer to left and right, an orientation that the theme of the Union of the Left or the 'plural Left' integrating the Communists seemed to have brought to perfection under Mitterrand. Today, Sarkozy has put to death the cadaverous form of Gaullism represented by Chirac. And on the part of the left, we have seen a collapse broadly heralded by the rout of Jospin in 2002, and still more so by the aberrant decision to vote for Chirac in the second round.[2]

What is of particular interest to us here is the disorientation brought about, in relation to the Right/Left system issuing from the 1940s, by the subjective and moral decomposition of the Socialist Party, and with it of the very notion of the 'Left', which for good reason adopts for its name a term of orientation, a topological term. It is clear that this notion was already in very poor shape, but with this election it has more or less finally perished. Already in the 1960s, Sartre said: 'The left is a stinking overturned corpse.' This was aggressive, but it was forty years ago. Let us say that matters have improved. This decomposition is not simply one of notable weakness in confrontation, of the political wretchedness evident now for a long while. Something fundamental, constitutive of the symbolism of French parliamentarism, has come to an end.

As always, of course, this is a long story. It really started with the inexorable crumbling of working-class virtues, and

2 [The second round of the presidential elections in 2002 was a run-off between Jacques Chirac for the right and Jean-Marie Le Pen for the far-right Front National, the Socialist candidate, Lionel Jospin, having been eliminated. The Socialist Party, like the crushing majority of the French left, called for a 'republican' vote for Chirac and against Le Pen. The former was elected with an enormous majority of 82 per cent. Badiou has an essay on this episode in *Polemics*.]

somewhat outside of the system of the Parti Communiste Français, thus already in the sixties of the last century, particularly in 1968 and perhaps even earlier. For a long while the PCF had already been showing disturbing signs of chauvinism, fear of any movement from A to Z that it did not control, and 'parliamentary cretinism' – to use a phrase from the nineteenth century, when the revolution was in better health. But even so, it kept in its vocabulary the dictatorship of the proletariat, which verbally set it apart from the 'democratic' consensus. From May 1968, besides becoming for a while the organized enemy of the entire revolutionary youth of students and workers, and the bulwark of the electoral and trade-union order, the PCF even sacrificed its verbal fetishes. It appeared as a cantankerous and egocentric form of the prevailing democracy. After which it allied itself with Mitterrand and started to disappear.

On the world scale, to be sure, there was the collapse of the USSR, accompanied by the loss of the 'Marxist' ideological bearings of which this worm-eaten state was the ostensible guardian. From this point of view, moreover, it is notable that what created the most serious crisis for the Left, in the face of the victorious pretensions of unleashed capitalism, was in no way Stalin. In Stalin's time, we have to admit, the political organizations of the workers and popular classes behaved infinitely better, and capitalism was that much less arrogant. There is simply no comparison. It was the liquidators – Brezhnev, the man of stagnation, and above all Gorbachev, the man of out-and-out reform – who plunged the world of the 'Left' into such a wretched state that no one knows when it will recover. Perhaps, moreover, the unqualified death of this reference point is desirable. We shall leave that question open.

Despite this complex archaeology detailing the Left's catastrophe, the election of Sarkozy remains nonetheless the mark of a new time, the advent of something disgusting, a blow against the symbolic structuring of French political life, in which the thematic of the Left, its constant recompositions and the possibility of its victory, was part of the familiar scenery of elections. It is this familiarity that has been attacked and defeated. But it is no consolation to you people of the Left that this is simply the end of a long process! From the moment when an old symbolic world received such a blow, you are completely disoriented. For this time round, the blow is not just the electoral figures, which were not so much worse than usual (47 per cent has for ages been the normal result for the Left); it strikes at the very frame of reference, the subjective law of counting.

What has characterized this election is that it has aggravated the disorientation, by revealing the intrinsically obsolete character of the whole frame of reference that arose from the last world war, the Left/Right system. What the election has brought to light is that the disorientation has reached the point at which the very system of orientation has been symbolically defeated. This is why Sarkozy, immediately after his election, can celebrate at Fouquet's and go off to Malta on a billionaire's yacht.[3] It's a way of saying: 'The Left no longer scares anyone; up with the rich, down with the poor!'

---

3 [Fouquet's is an expensive bar and restaurant, opened in 1899, on the Champs-Elysées. Traditionally the location for the after-party for the Césars ceremony (French equivalent of the Oscars), it was also where Nicolas Sarkozy and his supporters celebrated his victory in the second round of the presidential elections on 6 May 2007. Further confirming his growing reputation for a certain *nouveau riche* vulgarity, Sarkozy then took a holiday in Malta on board the luxurious yacht owned by his friend, the millionaire businessman Vincent Bolloré.]

Those sincere people of the Left who are still around, therefore, are seized with an uncontrollable nostalgia for the age of clear directions. Oh, how they regret all of the past! Mitterrand! De Gaulle! Even Georges Marchais! And even Chirac, the Brezhnev of Gaullism, who knew that doing nothing is the best way to die slowly. Indeed, they actually voted for Chirac, against Le Pen. Le Pen? Someone else from the old world. With Sarkozy and his gang in power, they'll even end up regretting that old scoundrel, mark my words. When Le Pen said 'Boo' there was a moment of fear, a nice demonstration, and everything was all right again. Nostalgia! Sarko's the president now, he'll put the screws on!

A very important symptom of this disorientation is the turncoats from the Left who have flocked to the Sarkozy camp. The Neuilly fidget was scarcely elected when we saw these rats from the 'Left', or supposedly such, running around everywhere.[4] The ships of the old world were abandoned on all sides, and very strange consultations went on in the corridors. A number of bigwigs of left opinion suddenly discovered Sarko's great virtues. That was even more disorienting. But it was only an advance sign of deeper movements. The rats signalled the first rumblings of an earthquake.

The underlying logic is after all the logic of the single party. This is exactly what our president has in mind: to gather everyone under his wing. It's only natural! Once the whole world accepts the capitalist order, the market

---

4 [After Sarkozy's election, he promoted a strategy of 'openness' vis-à-vis certain individuals of the Socialist Party, some of whom (such as Bernard Kouchner, Fadéla Amara, Eric Besson, and Martin Hirsch) joined the government, whilst others (such as Jacques Attali and Jack Lang) were appointed as leading members of various commissions.]

economy and representative democracy, these facts being equally objective and indubitable as universal gravitation, if not more, why carry on with the fiction of opposing parties? My friend the Slovenian philosopher Slavoj Žižek has said somewhere that what was not understood, when Stalinism and parliamentary democracy were counterposed to one another, was that Stalinism was the future of parliamentary democracy. We are getting there, slowly and tortuously. There will be an acceleration; there already is. After all, the technological means for controlling the population are already such that Stalin, with his endless handwritten files, his mass executions, his spies with hats, his gigantic lice-ridden camps and bestial tortures, appears like an amateur from another age. That is another reason why it is hard to imagine our president in the role of the Georgian – as guide or 'little father' of his people. How could he manage this with the image of a middle-rank executive at a second-rate bank? And yet, in his bouncy, chatterbox, improvised way, we may be able to say one day that Sarkozy aimed to be the great builder of our single party, the Union for Presidential Unanimity or UPU. For this to succeed, it is enough that the turncoats who have rallied to him, the rats who have left the sinking ship of the left, steadily constitute a flow, a tide, a tsunami of rats. Empirically, of course, things will certainly not proceed on this scale in the months to come. But we are already there symbolically. A certain number of personalities represent this posture, this possibility – the avant-garde rats for the construction of Sarkozy's UPU. Indeed, all they are doing is extending, completing and giving a definitive form to the broad movement of counter-revolutionary renegacy that began in 1976 with the clique of the 'new philosophers'.

You will certainly have noted how in the wake of his election victory Sarkozy hammered home the point that he was now the president of us all. I certainly didn't ask him to be my president. It was he who said it: he wants to be the organizer of us all, a worthy representative of the future single party. And for the moment, against this grandiose project, there is nothing else on a mass level but nostalgia for the old world, the world of right and left, of the legitimate demands of the workers, of social security, well-organized civil servants, secular schoolteachers, and finally the French countryside, its villages, its quiet strength . . . Registering the blow inflicted on us provokes an intense and depressive nostalgia for the traditional old world, French charm and its markers of subjective orientation.

The third element, after the components of impulse and nostalgia, is clearly a component of impotence. We can even say, a presentation, a subjective representation, of impotence. It is not that a new impotence has arisen. 'What in God's name can we do?' has been a desperate question for a good number of people for quite a while. But this time there is a very clear and focused representation of impotence. This impotence was effective, it is now acknowledged, and I believe – optimistically – that it is acknowledged as an intrinsic dimension of electoral democracy. This is undoubtedly why the blow we have experienced is severe. Electoral democracy acknowledges the extent to which it is a site where impotence is the rule, the impotence of those who try to govern their actions and passions by the idea that, after all, the real is rational. Everyone can see that electoral democracy is not a space of real choice, but something that registers, like a passive seismograph, propensities that are quite different from an enlightened intention, and have nothing in common with the representation that a real thought can have of the objectives that the will pursues.

It is very striking – and even a matter of surprise and consternation, despite their unanimity on this point – to see how politicians and commentators have immediately empha-sized as the decisive element the numerical significance of the electoral turnout. They did not say, as might have been reasonable: 'Many people voted, and we might well wonder why, given what was on offer.' No, they said: 'A great victory for democracy.' But suppose, in another context and another time (I deliberately take this shop-worn and ridiculous comparison), an enormous number of people had voted, say, for Hitler (as indeed happened), that the electors turned out en masse to do this; would we have spoken of a crushing victory for democracy? Only in a very special sense! If numbers alone are a cause for celebration, then this means that democracy is strictly indifferent to any content – that it represents nothing more than its own form, the display of a numerical element. In these emphatic proclamations, any reflection – possibly gloomy – on what people did is done away with. I think that anyone who praises this copious voting must share the general depression. It assumes that these ridiculous voters cannot even be criticized. We can't even say: 'If it was only to give us the fidgety mayor of Neuilly, they would have done better to stay at home.' We are supposed to rejoice abstractly that people came out to vote en masse. Certainly, this only organized a disaster, of which we shall suffer the calamitous consequences, but all glory to them! By their stupid number, they brought the triumph of democracy. In sum, the depression also arises from the necessity that all 'democrats' find themselves in to maintain that people have got what they wanted, that the result is unchallengeable, and there is nothing more to be done. That is already what all the politicians rushed to say on the very night of the poll. They all said: 'Please note, we certainly respect universal suffrage.' They are more 'respectful' than I am of the 'popular will', even when they see it as idiotic and dangerous. Bow down before the numbers!

I must tell you that I absolutely do not respect universal suffrage in itself; it depends on what it does. Is universal suffrage the only thing we should respect, regardless of what it produces? And why is that? In no other field of action and judgement on actions do we consider something to be valid independently of its actual effects. Universal suffrage has produced a number of abominations. In history, competent majorities have legitimated Hitler and Pétain, the Algerian war, the invasion of Iraq . . . There is nothing innocent, therefore, about 'democratic majorities'. To praise numbers because people came out to vote, independently of the result, and to respect this majority decision in a proclaimed indifference to its content, is another symptom of the general depression. Because if you cannot even express your disgust at the result, if you are obliged to respect it, then at least please realize what you are doing! Not only should we note the recurring stupidity of numbers, at the same time we should have the greatest respect for them. It's too much!

In actual fact, what we sense here, without people really being able to articulate it, is that elections are at least as much an instrument of repression as the instrument of expression that they claim to be. Nothing produces greater satisfaction on the part of the oppressors than to hold elections everywhere, to impose them, by war if need be, on people who did not ask for them. Our president has not failed to say, about strikes for example, that we'd better look out. Thanks to Sarkozy, strikes will be terribly electoral, they'll need an absolute majority, with secret ballots, court officials at the ballot box, and so on. Is this designed to 'democratize' strikes? Like hell it is! It is to make them as difficult as possible, under the pretence that all this is to protect the rights of the user.[5] On this point, in any case, we should remember May '68. There were millions of strikers, demonstrations every day, an unprecedented alliance between young people on different trajectories, workers and students. The whole world was seized by the tremendous novelty of the situation. Red flags could even be seen in certain fashionable districts! Everywhere enthusiasm, in other words, everywhere the hope for an end to enslavement. And then, all that those in power needed, in other words de Gaulle and particularly Pompidou, was to organize elections, and we had the most massively reactionary parliament since 1919, a real 'sky-blue chamber'. It is beyond question that the election was the essential recourse to dissolve and crush the movement. And it was certainly not out of extremism, but in the fullest lucidity, that the activists of the time cried out in the streets: 'Elections, a con trick!' I am not saying that elections are repressive

5 The idea that 'users' are systematically hostile to strikes is a well-established untruth, one among so many adduced as evidence by the dominant politicians and media. The very long strike by railwaymen in December 1995, for example, was supported throughout the country with massive demonstrations, even more so than the strikes of May 1968. In certain provincial towns (Roanne, for example), half of the total population took part in protest marches! And there have been several other similar cases since then. The same goes for the tireless mantra of the reactionaries that 'there are too many state employees'; it is a complete fiction that people share this idea. A recent poll shows that, out of all the equally detestable proposals of Sarkozy in his full 'state of grace', the one about rapidly reducing the number of state employees has received least support.

in essence. Simply that they are incorporated into a form of state, the capitalist-parliamentary state, appropriate for the maintenance of the established order, and that they consequently always have a conservative function, which in case of troubles becomes a repressive one. All this, which today is displayed in the clearest possible fashion, provokes an increased feeling of impotence. If the space of state decision only leaves us ordinary citizens with the vote, then it is not easy to see, at least at the present time, what routes are open for a politics of emancipation.

And so, at the end of these reflections, I believe that we can analyse the subjective situation of the remains of the Left in France, and more generally of men and women of goodwill, under the effect of Sarkozy's triumph, as one of historical nostalgia and acknowledged impotence.

I thus explain the perception that I have of you this evening, my diagnosis if you like, as a depressive asthenia. This is the time to draw on the definition that Lacan gives of the analytic cure. Since we are all depressed, a cure is needed. Lacan said that the object of the cure is 'to raise impotence to impossibility'. If we are suffering from a syndrome whose worst symptom is acknowledged impotence, then we can raise this impotence to impossibility. But what does that actually mean? A number of things. It means finding a real point to hold on to, whatever the cost. It means no longer being in the vague net of impotence, historical nostalgia and the depressive component, but rather finding, constructing and holding on to a real point, which we know we are going to hold on to, precisely because it is a point uninscribable in the law of the situation, unanimously declared by the prevailing opinion to be both (and contradictorily) absolutely deplorable and completely impracticable, but which you yourselves declare that you are going to hold on to, whatever the cost; you are then in a position to raise impotence to impossibility. If you hold on to a point such as this, then you become a subject bound to the consequences of what is unanimously held to be a crazy disaster and happily quite impossible, but to which you grant reality and thereby make yourselves an exception to the depressive syndrome.

The whole question is: What does 'holding on' to a real point of this kind mean, supposing it can be found? Holding on to a point means exposing the individual animal that one is to becoming the subject of the consequences of this point. It means incorporating oneself into the construction of these consequences, into the subjective body that they gradually constitute in our world. In this way, we construct, in the temporality of opinion, a different duration, distinct from that which we have been driven into by the symbolization of the state.

If you are prisoners of the temporality of opinion, you are going to say, like so many of the Socialist Party bosses or electors: 'For God's sake! We had to put up with Chirac for twelve years, and now we have to wait again for the next time round! Seventeen years! Perhaps twenty-two! A whole lifetime! It's not possible!' And then, at best you get depressed; at worst you become a rat. The rat is the person who, internal to the temporality of opinion, cannot stand to wait. The next time round, as ordered by the state, is very far away. I'll be old, says the rat. He doesn't want to stew in impotence, but even less so in impossibility! The impossible offers very little sustenance to him.

We have to recognize that Sarkozy is deeply acquainted with the subjectivity of rats. He is a virtuoso at attracting them. Perhaps he was a rat himself? In 1995, when he was in too much of a hurry for a real ministerial position, and betrayed Chirac for Balladur?[6] In any case, by finding a state use for rat psychology, he deserves a name that is famous in the annals of psychoanalysis. I propose therefore to call Nicolas Sarkozy the Rat Man. Yes, that suits him, it's well deserved.

The rat is the person who needs to rush in to the duration on offer, not being in any state to construct a different one. The point we need to find must be one able to annex a different duration. Being neither a rat nor a depressive means constructing a different time from that which the state, or the state of things, assigns us. An impossible time, therefore, but a time that is *ours*.

This is the moment to return again to the history of May '68. And the declaration of our president about May '68, at a big election meeting, was really very interesting. We should understand properly what he was trying to say, that putting an end to May '68 once and for all was the supreme goal of his action, of that 'rupture' that he proclaimed. I admit that I find this declaration rather obscure. There is something deep about it. It's different from the usual economic and ecological playacting (the budget balance, executives' pay, the hole in social security funding, the hole in the state pension fund, the ozone hole, all those holes we are obsessed by), but it is obscure. As far as we professional *soixante-huitards* are concerned, our impression was that

6 [For a long time, Sarkozy was a favourite of Jacques Chirac but, in an act that the latter and his supporters would never forgive, Sarkozy supported Edouard Balladur, the rival centre-right candidate in the first round of the presidential elections of 1995. Chirac won in both the first and second rounds, consigning Balladur to the political margins, but his former protégé was henceforth forever tarred with the brush of treachery.]

unfortunately May '68 came to an end a long time ago. What does Sarkozy, the Rat Man, know that we don't? Is there something that pushes him to see the fundamental objective of his action in May 2007, four whole decades later, being to put an end to May '68? For the Rat Man, it seems, May '68 is still with us – and that's good news! Let us hope it is true, and that May '68 is still alive in minds and situations, present and to come. Mao was in the habit of saying that 'the eye of the peasant sees right'. Let's hope that, at least as far as May '68 is concerned, this is true of the eye of the Rat Man! For if May '68 really is for the new state reactionaries the burning question of the day, if May '68 is still really alive, we can say: 'Thank you kindly, that's very good to hear, we hadn't realized.'

Let's be serious, then, and try to interpret what 'May '68' can mean today, for a servant of the stock-exchange index, a confirmed enemy of undocumented workers and the youngsters of the housing estates, a man obsessed by policing, and a prolific author of repressive laws. He tells us: May '68 was the time when people stopped making a clear distinction between Good and Evil. Sarkozy, in other words, has a Nietzschean vision of May '68. And yet May '68 was the very opposite! It was in no way 'beyond good and evil'. On the contrary, it was a precise identification of evil: Evil, for the rebel activists of the red decade, between 1966 and 1976, meant the men of finance and power who resembled the Rat Man. Basically, *he* is Evil. And Good was the politicized worker, the peoples in revolt, the revolutionary activists. May '68 proposed, quite the opposite to what Sarkozy tells us, a very clear and strong division between Good and Evil. Sarkozy is not seriously talking about May '68. His diatribe merely symbolizes a moralizing

37

propaganda. I shall return, moreover, to the role of morality in this affair, the 'moral crisis' of our country, and so on. These are the discourses that should be closely analysed in philosophical terms. Let us rest content for the moment by asking: What does the Rat Man have in mind with his absurd moral diatribe about Good and Evil? What is the spectre haunting him under the name of May '68 – to take up Derrida's analysis in his book on the spectres of Marx? In fact, when Marx wrote in 1848 that 'a spectre is haunting Europe', he meant that communism – the name of the spectre – was the terrible obsession of the bourgeoisie. And when Sarkozy admits that May '68 is the spectre haunting him, which he wants to shake off, he is basically speaking of one of the last real manifestations of the spectre of communism, and what he says is (permit me here to paraphrase the Rat Man): 'We modern reactionaries no longer want to be haunted by anything at all. We are going to definitively eradicate any idea that assumes it is possible to hold on to a real point outside the law of the state, outside the constraints of the world that we dominate. In May '68, some people told us that they would hold on to such a real point, for example a completely new alliance between young intellectuals and workers, and they tried as much as they could to hold on to this right to the end. We cannot support anyone even entertaining the idea of this, let alone the reality. We want to root out the very possibility of thinking that this kind of obstinacy in holding on to a real point is possible. We want, in other words, the disappearance of the spectre to be publicly and unanimously recognized. Empirical communism has disappeared, which is all well and good, but that is not enough. We want to prevent anyone mentioning communism – which is the generic name of our defeat and indeed our disappearance – even in the form of a hypothesis.'

Yes indeed, the eye of the Rat Man sees right. We may discuss exactly what were the points that the activists and demonstrators of the red years sought to hold on to. What is certain is that these all referred to the Communist hypothesis in a generic sense: to move beyond capitalism, private property, financial circulation, the despotic state, and so on. Were they aptly chosen or not, genuinely new or still too heavily marked by the old? That is a discussion among to hold among ourselves, as contemporary upholders of the spectre of communism, and not a discussion with the Rat Man. And yet, there is reason to think that there was something threatening there (for him and his kind), something that started up and developed around 1965, and lasted as a mass phenomenon until around 1975, something that indicated a new discipline and a new abnegation, that of a real point held in a kind of joyous indifference to the political and commercial law of the world that otherwise prevails on all sides.

If this election was important, it is because it bore the conviction shared by those who are now in power, as well as all those who want to follow them, that perhaps an end could be made of this 'something' of which May '68 is one of the names, the most recent to appear in France. And how can this be done? By making sure that the metamorphosis of passive and stereotyped consuming individuals into subjects of a real process, in which holding on to some point is the rule, is – in the strict sense – outside the law. Not only in the police sense, though this will certainly also happen. But in the sense that this metamorphosis will belong forever to the order of the unrepresentable absolute. To do 'something' that is not internal to the temporality offered us would then fall not just outside the law of the empirical world, but outside the law of any possible or imaginable world.

If we were to suppose this operation accomplished (and that is what is meant by 'putting an end to May '68'), then the temptation to submit would become overwhelming. For holding on to an 'illegal' point is the only thing that stands in an authentic dialectic with the negative impulse, the experience of depression. If there is not such a point, then the only liveable (or survivable) outcome is the most abject submission to reality. We find ourselves here in a Lacanian dialectic, between the Real and reality. If nothing punctures a hole in reality, if nothing is an exception to it, if no point can be held on to for its own sake whatever it costs, then there is only the reality and submission to this reality, what Lacan called 'the service of wealth [*le service des biens*]'. And the violence against May '68 seeks to preserve the unqualified hegemony of this 'service of wealth'. As we know, the service of wealth is the service of those who have wealth. Sarkozy's famous escapade on the billionaire's yacht – right after the high-society booze-up at Fouquet's on the night of his victory – was in no way a mistake, a fault, as it has sometimes been presented. Certainly, he went to see his commanders, his sponsors, the high financiers whose vassal he is. But above all he declared to the whole world that this is the way things would now be: there's nothing better than personal gain, everything is now under the rule of the service of wealth. This is the only rule of this world, which is made up through and through by the circulation of capital. What will you say against it? Anyone who does not have a real point, precisely a point of exception to the rule, a point in the name of which they speak universally in a disinterested way, has nothing to say in response. If the service of wealth is the law of the world, why not let it take hold of you too? Sarkozy has symbolically shown that he helped himself by helping those with wealth and that this is why he was elected – that he was elected by a mass of simpletons. As for those who are not in a position to help themselves by helping the service of wealth, so much the worse for them. They could have rejected the idea that 'the service of wealth' should be the world's motto. They could have abstained from voting, and especially from voting for the Rat Man.

We can now draw a certain conclusion. To raise impotence to impossibility means rejecting the service of wealth, which is the impotence of the possible. It thus means choosing a point that is *your* point, and that you say you will hold on to, whatever it costs, against the law of the world. What point, then? Never mind what, as long as it is formally an exception to the rule of the service of wealth, and universally proposes a truth discipline.

3 Eight Points, to Start With

.

Since everything, in the world whose emblem is Sarkozy, rests on holding firmly on to some point, let us be extravagant. I shall put you on the track of eight practicable points. This is neither a programme nor a list, but rather a table of possibilities, naturally abstract and incomplete.

Point 1. *Assume that all workers labouring here belong here, and must be treated on a basis of equality, and respected accordingly – indeed honoured – especially workers of foreign origin.*

This is an essential question, its direct consequence having a scope whose various dimensions have not yet been fully explored: to re-establish the signifier 'worker' in the speech and action of politics. Not, indeed, in the line that prevailed in the nineteenth century, that of the first epoch of the communist hypothesis (the working class, motive element of the natural historical movement towards the emancipation of humanity as a whole). Nor in that prevalent in the twentieth century, that of the second epoch of the communist hypothesis (the party of the working class, unique and indispensable leadership for revolutionary politics, and then exclusive organ of the dictatorship of the proletariat, in the form of party-state). But in a third line that is still at an experimental stage: 'worker' as the generic name for all who can withdraw themselves, in an organized way, from the realized hegemony of financial capital and its servants.

In the immediate experience of this question, the organization of workers of foreign origin occupies a strategic position. We already learn this from the schemes of that 'teacher by negative example' – as the Chinese Communists used to say – that is parliamentary politics. Control immigration, send people back home, make them learn French three years in advance, ban family reunion, expel school students, restrict then abolish the right of asylum; then we have wretched 'civilizing' campaigns against the customs of people who arrive in our country, aggressive and constraining feminism, a secularism of exclusion and repression in dress, informing and police raids . . . These constant campaigns show us what is the principal target for the enemy, in all its shades (the Socialists, since the 1980s at least, set the tone), and consequently the place for our own action.

Let us start by saying, and this would be your fixed point: 'Workers of foreign origin must be recognized by the state as free subjects. They must actually be honoured as such. Let us construct a set of procedures that not only aim to protect these workers, these families and these children, but also organize them as a popular political power so that everyone, even if only from a healthy fear of their strength, considers them as free subjects and a tribute to this country. Yes, they should be honoured. We, at all events, have far more reason for honouring a Malian who does the dishes in a Chinese restaurant, takes part after his endless work in meetings and interventions and thereby becomes an organic intellectual of the new politics, than we do for honouring the Rat Man.

'Let us talk the language of Nietzsche. We have to be able to incorporate ourselves into a movement of the trans-valuation of established values. There are moments when one must be able to assert a reversal of imposed appearances. We must have the liberty to say, wagering on the thought and action of politics, that many of those who are persecuted should absolutely be honoured – not because they are perse-cuted (that is the abomination of humanitarianism and charity, the opium of the petty bourgeoisie), but because in the name of us all they organize the assertion of a different conception of human life. This was Marx's own gesture: these workers, who have nothing and are considered the dangerous class, I am going to honour, and actively take part in organizing them (the First International), inasmuch as they are the collective motor of the history of emancipa-tion, the main builders of an egalitarian society. In whatever new ways we can repeat this gesture today, we shall do so. We shall reject the verdict of Sarkozy and his rats, declaring from the height of his reactionary insignificance that the Malian dishwasher is no more than tolerated, and must fulfil a countless number of conditions simply to be allowed to remain where he is. We shall construct, at variance with the time of public opinion, a collective duration within which not only will the Malian dishwasher gain recognition as a free subject, but he will be particularly honoured.'

There is no lack of support for holding on to this point.[1]

---

1 As an effective example of this point, we can refer to the proposals and actions of the Rassemblement des Collectifs des Ouvriers Sans Papiers des Foyers. Write to *Le Journal Politique*, c/o Le Perroquet, BP 84, 75642 Paris cedex 10. See the Web site: *orgapoli.net*.

Point 2. *Art as creation, whatever its epoch and nationality, is superior to culture as consumption, no matter how contemporary.*

There are a number of places where the validity and pertinence of this point can be asserted. The media and the schools, in particular. Maintaining, for example, that *The Tale of Genji*, written in eleventh-century Japan by Lady Murasaki Shikibu, is immeasurably superior to all the Goncourt prize-winners of the last thirty years. Or that there is no reason why students, even in the first form of secondary school, should be offered Marcel Pagnol's *La Gloire de mon père* rather than *La Princesse de Clèves*. We should also make clear that it is ridiculous to place on the same level, in the name of the uniformity of what are called 'musics', musical comedy, easy listening, the folklore of distant islands, peasant dances, African drumming, Boulez, Messiaen or Ferneyhough. Music for entertainment, moreover, should be judged in terms of genuine music, and not the other way round; and in the last analysis, music of the past should be judged by the standard of today's creations, as nothing better displays the contemporary reactionary desire than to wax ecstatic, like the fans of 'baroque', over the works of a seventeenth-century prig rediscovered under a well-deserved coat of dust in the Montpelier library and interpreted with the aid of shrill 'original instruments', while the greatest masterpieces of the twentieth century are not played.

Point 3. *Science, which is inherently free, is absolutely superior to technology, even and especially when the technology is profitable.*

To organize and struggle around this point is highly important, especially in relation to research institutions, educational programmes and accounts that the press gives of new scientific developments. The universal and generic validity of scientific discovery, not commensurable with technological profitability, is a point that must be reasserted today, with higher mathematics as the central paradigm, as Plato saw it, and it is crucial to reaffirm, against the selective and aristocratic organization of mathematics, that this quite uniquely belongs to all by virtue of the very clarity of its pure thought.

You are doubtless familiar with the declarations of the Rat Man on the subject of ancient literature. This is an example that also holds good for those disciplines without known applications. He said, in substance: 'You are free to study ancient literature if you want to, but don't ask the state to pay for that privilege. The taxpayers' money must go to computing and economics.' This is one of countless quotations by this character that show him literally on his knees before profits and profiteers. Our president develops a whole ontology of profit: what isn't profitable has no reason for existence, and if some cranks are still attached to gratuitous mental activities, let them look after themselves. They won't get a bean!

Holding on to this point means that what has a universal value, and thus maintains a relationship with those truths that humanity is capable of, is in no way homogeneous with what has a market value. It is of the utmost importance that what has universal value is restored to its due place, the first place, and honoured as such. The question of the value of science links up here with that of political values. The creators of higher mathematics should be honoured like those workers who, despite all the unbelievable difficulties of their existence, very often speak four or five languages, have come here to perform tasks that no one else wants to do, and even so find the time to engage in political invention. You are the people who wash the dishes in restaurants, who clean the streets, who dig holes in the road, and on top of this you hold unprecedented meetings – we shall at least honour you for that. The same is true for the sciences. Whatever relates to the essential gratuitousness of intellectual activity, being both difficult and illuminating, should be supported and honoured in its very essence, against the norm of profitable technological application.

We should do justice to Auguste Comte, who saw very well that the future of humanity required an unprecedented alliance between the proletarians and scientific thought (and also Woman, but that brings us to the next point).

Point 4. *Love must be reinvented (what we can call the 'Rimbaud point'), but also quite simply defended.*

Love, a truth procedure bearing on the Two as such, on difference *qua* difference, is threatened on all sides. It is threatened from the Left, if I can use that term here, by libertinage, which reduces it to variations on the theme of sex, and, from the right, by the liberal conception that subordinates it to contract. Libertarians and liberals focus their ruinous and combined offensives on love. The former champion the rights of the democratic individual to pleasure in all its forms, without seeing that, in a world governed by the dictatorship of the market, they serve as trailblazers for pornography, which is one of the largest planetary industries. The latter see love as a contract between two free and equal individuals, which comes down to wondering whether the advantages that one person obtains equitably balance those obtained by the other. In each case, we remain within the doctrine according to which everything that exists is a matter of arbitration between individual interests. The only difference between libertarians and liberals, who both take the satisfaction of individuals as their only norm, is that the former refer to desire, whereas the latter refer to demand.

We maintain, against this view of things, that love begins beyond desire and demand, even though it embraces these. It is an examination of the world from the point of the Two, with the result that its territory is in no way the individual. If love has a subject, it is precisely because it is a disciplined construction that cannot be reduced either to the satisfaction of desire, or to an egalitarian contract between responsible individuals. Love is violent, irresponsible and creative. Its duration is irreducible to that of private satisfactions. It creates a new thought, whose unified content bears on disjunction and its consequences. To hold on to the point of love is educational as to the mutilation that the supposed sovereignty of the individual imposes on human existence. Love teaches in fact that the individual as such is something vacuous and insignificant. Already by itself, this teaching demands love be considered a noble and difficult cause in contemporary times.

Point 5. *Any sick person who asks for a doctor to treat them should be examined and treated as well as possible, in the present conditions of medicine as the doctor understands these, and unconditionally with respect to age, nationality, 'culture', administrative status or financial resources (this is the Hippocratic point).*

It is a question here of giving back its full force to a Greek maxim, the 'Hippocratic oath', which is old and correct, but today has been completely wiped off the slate. Today, before treating a patient, it is first necessary to consider the state of the economy, the funds of the hospital, the hierarchy of services, the origin of the patient, whether they are black or white, their resources, identity papers, and so on. The question of health and the medical function is in the process of being totally absorbed by budgetary considerations, the border police and social discrimination. This goes well beyond the very real threats that weigh on our national system of funding health-care services, which – to the great chagrin of the rats of all kinds – is considered the best in the world. It bears on the very definition of medicine. A very large number of practitioners today, especially in the hospital hierarchy, have turned themselves into agents or accomplices of a bureaucratic management that increasingly practises an intolerable segregation. This is why they must be reminded most energetically of the Hippocratic oath.

Point 6. *Any process that is intended to serve as a fragment of a politics of emancipation must be held superior to any managerial necessity.*

To add a single brief comment on this: we have particularly to assert this superiority when the managerial constraint is declared to be 'modern', and is claimed to result from a 'necessary concern to reform the country' and 'put an end to archaic practices'. It is a question of the impossible, in other words the real, which alone lifts us out of impotence. 'Modernization', as we see every day, is the name for a strict and servile definition of the possible. These 'reforms' invariably aim at making impossible what used to be practicable (for the largest number), and making profitable (for the dominant oligarchy) what did not use to be so. As against the managerial definition of the possible, we must assert that what we are going to do, though held by the agents of this management to be impossible, is in reality, at the very point of this impossibility, no more than the creation of a possibility previously unperceived and universally valid.

Point 7. *A newspaper that belongs to rich managers does not have to be read by someone who is neither a manager nor rich.*

That is just a very small point, but applicable right away. Just look at what these newspapers, as well as the most popular television channels, really are. They belong to the king of concrete, the prince of luxury products, the emperor of military aircraft, the magnate of celebrity magazines, the water millionaire . . . In other words, to all those people who, on their yachts or their estates, take little Sarkozy, who has done so well, on their hospitable knees. How can we accept this state of affairs? Why should the broad mass of people be at the mercy of the price of concrete mixers, or the world market for ostrich skin, when it comes to getting information? Stop reading those papers. Look at sources that originate elsewhere than in the dominant commercial circuits. Let the ultra-rich newspaper proprietors talk to themselves. Let us withdraw our interest from the interests that their self-interest wants to make ours.

Point 8. *There is only one world.*

This point is so important that I shall now devote a whole chapter to it.

4   Only One World

Contemporary capitalism, as we all know, prides itself on its global nature. Globalization is the buzzword on all sides. The enemies of this globalization say that they want a different world: they speak of 'alter-globalization'. So the world is no longer simply the place where people exist, it is also the stake in a political battle. The question is 'what world?', and this is actually a twofold question. There is the analytical question: What world(s) are we living in? And then the normative question: What world do we want to live in?

The practical connection between the analytical question and the normative question gives a definition of current politics: a politics that proposes the means for moving from the world as it is now to the world as we would wish it to be. Alter-globalization, ecology, democracy, sustainable development, the defence of human rights – all these practices seem to define various forms of politics on the global stage.

This is very clear as it stands, if we can truly say today that there is a single world. But is this really the case? The answer is complex. First of all, unleashed capitalism declares that its norms, in particular what it calls 'democracy' and 'freedoms', must become those of the whole world, and that this is in the process of happening thanks to the efforts of the 'international community' in general – a rather weird subject this 'community', we might say in passing, above all when it is confused with the servility of the bureaucracy known as the UN – and the efforts of the 'civilized' nations in particular, i.e. the USA and its clientele. Second, it is clear that the same unleashed capitalism seeks to impose the political conviction that there are two separate worlds and not just one. There is the world of the rich and powerful, and the immense world of the excluded, subjected and persecuted. This contradiction makes us suspicious of the reality of globalization, and of the politics that appeal to this – whether for or against. It may well be that the political question is not 'How are we to build the world that we desire, within and against the "democratic" and capitalist world?', but rather 'How are we to assert the existence of a single world, the indivisible world of all living people, when it is asserted, often by violence, that such a world does not exist?'[1] A question of existence, in other words, and not a question of character. Before any concern for the 'quality of life', after the fashion of the replete citizens of the protected world, it is necessary first of all to live, as billions of human animals are desperately seeking to do – elsewhere, but increasingly here as well.

Why am I justified in saying that the real axiom of the

---

1 The thesis that 'there is only one world' underlies the mass action of the group 'Collective politique Sida en Afrique: la France doit fournir les traitements', whose journal is *Pays intervention fleuve*. More information can be found on the site: www.entretemps.asso.fr/Sida.

dominant politics is that the unified world of human subjects does not exist? Because the world that is declared to exist and that supposedly has to be imposed on everyone, the world of globalization, is uniquely a world of objects and monetary signs, a world of the free circulation of products and financial flows. It is precisely the world foreseen by Marx a hundred and fifty years ago: the world of the global market. All that exist in this world are things – objects for sale – and signs – the abstract instruments of sale and purchase, the various forms of money and credit. But it is not true that human subjects freely exist in this world. To start with, they totally lack the basic right to move around and settle where they wish. In their crushing majority, the women and men of the supposed 'world', the world of commodities and money, have no access at all to this world. They are rigorously locked out of it, where there are very few commodities for them and no money at all. 'Locked out' here is very specific. Walls are being constructed all over the world – the wall designed to separate Palestinians and Israelis, the border wall between Mexico and the United States, the electric fence between Africa and the Spanish enclaves. The mayor of an Italian town has proposed building a wall between the town centre and the suburbs! Walls everywhere, to make sure that the poor remain locked in their place. Not to mention prison walls, prisons having become for the rich a big and profitable industry, where millions of poor or semi-poor are cooped up, cast there by an ever more ferocious activity of police and courts, and particularly young people, very often black, Arab, Latino . . .

It is almost twenty years since the Berlin Wall fell. The press and politicians of the 'free' world chanted that this was a symbol of planetary unity after seventy years of division. During these seventy years it was clear that there were two worlds: the socialist world and the capitalist world – or, as it used to be put, the totalitarian world and the democratic world. The fall of the Berlin Wall was supposedly the triumph of a single world, the world of democracy. Today, however, we can see that the wall was only shifted. It used to run between the totalitarian East and the democratic West; today it divides the rich capitalist North from the devastated and poor South, and more generally the protected territories of the beneficiaries of the established order from the rough ground where the others settle as best they can. Within the so-called developed countries, as they are still called, the recognized political contradiction used to oppose a working class, which was sometimes strong and organized, to a dominant bourgeoisie that controlled the state. Today we have side by side the rich beneficiaries of world commerce and the enormous mass of excluded.

'Excluded' is the name for all those who are not in the real world but outside it, behind the wall and the barbed wire, whether they are peasants in villages of millennial poverty, or urban dwellers in favelas, *banlieues*, estates, hostels, squats and shantytowns. Until roughly the 1990s, there was an ideological wall, a political iron curtain; today there is a wall separating the pleasures of wealth from the desire of the poor. It is just as if, in order for the single world of objects and monetary signs to exist, living bodies had to be separated according to their origin and their resources.

There is no single world of human beings, in the precise sense that, behind the propaganda about globalization, the thesis that governs an increasingly violent and enclosed politics is that there are two worlds at least. The price of the supposedly unified world of Capital is this brutal and violent division of human existence into two regions separated by walls, police dogs, bureaucratic controls, naval patrols, barbed wire and expulsions.

Why has what the politicians and the servile press of the Western countries call the 'problem of immigration' – an expression that in France derives from Le Pen – become in all these countries a fundamental datum of state policy? Because all the foreigners who arrive, live and work here are proof that the thesis of a democratic unity of the world realized by the market and the 'international community' is a complete sham. If it were true, we would have to welcome these 'foreigners' as people coming from the same world as ourselves. We would have to treat them as we treat someone from another region who stops over in our town, then finds work and settles there. But this is not at all what happens. The most widespread conviction, and that which government policies constantly seek to reinforce, is that *these people come from a different world*. That is the problem. They are the living proof that our democratic and developed world is not, for those in charge of the dominant capitalist order, the only world of women and men. There exist in our midst women and men who, although they live and work here like anyone else, are considered all the same to have come from another world. Money is the same everywhere, the dollar or euro are the same, and the dollars or euros that these foreigners from another world have are happily accepted by everyone. But as for these people themselves, because of their origin and their mode of existence we are repeatedly told that they are not part of our world. The state authorities and their blind followers will keep tabs on them, ban them from staying, mercilessly criticize their customs, their way of dressing, their family or religious practices. Many people, inspired by fear and organized in this fear by the state, anxiously wonder how many of them there are among us, how many people who come from another world. Tens of thousands? Millions? A horrible question, when you think about it. A question that inevitably leads to persecution, prohibition and expulsion on a mass scale. A question that, in other circumstances, paved the way for extermination.

We know perfectly well today that, if the unity of the world is a unity of objects and monetary signs, there is no such unity for living bodies, for all the talk of democracy. Instead there are zones, walls, desperate journeys, contempt and death. This is why the central political question today is indeed that of the world, the existence of the world.

Many would see this as an expansion of democracy. We have to extend to the whole world the right form of world, that which we have in the Western democracies or Japan. But this vision is absurd. The absolute material basis of the Western democratic world is the free circulation of objects and monetary signs. Its most fundamental subjective maxim is competition, the free competition that imposes the supremacy of wealth and the instruments of power. The inevitable result of obeying this maxim is the separation of living beings by and for the bitter defence of the privileges of wealth and power.

We are familiar today with the concrete form of this 'expansion' of democracy to which the 'international community' – the coalition of the planet's gendarme states

– is so devoted. It is, quite simply, war. War in Palestine, in Iraq, in Afghanistan, in Somalia, in much of Africa . . . The fact that long wars are needed in order to organize elections should lead us to reflect not just on war, but on elections as well. What conception of the world does electoral democracy rest on today? After all, this democracy imposes the law of numbers, just as the world unified by commodities imposes the monetary law of numbers. It might well be that the imposition of electoral numbers by war, as done in Baghdad or Kabul, leads back to our present problem: if the world is one of objects and signs, it is a world in which everything is counted. And those who do not count, or are poorly counted, have our laws of counting imposed on them by war. Besides, if the law of counting gives a result different from the results we expect, we additionally impose, by police violence and war, not just counting, but the 'right' count, one that ensures that democracy must elect democrats, in other words docile pro-American clients and no one else. As we have seen when Westerners, with certain of our intellectuals in the lead, applauded the interruption of the electoral process in Algeria which gave a victory to the 'Islamists', or when the same people refused to recognize the crushing electoral victory of Hamas in the Palestinian territories. These same Westerners did not hesitate to mount a military operation to force the resignation and exile of the regularly elected President Aristide of Haiti, who enjoyed an absolute majority support in public opinion. Not to mention that Hezbollah's majority in southern Lebanon does not prevent it being termed a 'terrorist' organization. In all four cases, this denial by the 'democracies' of their own norms of counting simply shows the truth of these norms: the perpetuation of the established capitalist order by parties that in the end are indistinguishable from one another, and the defence of this perpetuation through war. For war is indeed the price of these electoral counts when they are simultaneously imposed and denied. Civil war and invasion in Palestine, atrocious civil war in Algeria, war of aggression in Lebanon, and the assiduous maintenance of various warlords across the African continent. All this proves that 'the world' thus conceived does not really exist. What exists is a false and closed world, artificially kept separate from general humanity by incessant violence.

The problem then has to be reversed. We cannot start from an analytical agreement on the existence of the world and proceed to a normative action about its characteristics. The disagreement, like all genuine disagreements, is not over qualities but over existences. Faced with the two artificial and deadly worlds of which the 'West' – that damned word! – names the disjunction, we must assert right at the start the existence of the single world, as an axiom and a principle. We must say this very simple sentence: 'There is only one world.' This is not an objective conclusion. We know that, under the law of money, there is not a single world of women and men. There is the wall that divides the rich and the poor. This sentence 'there is only one world' is performative. It is we who decide that this is how it is for us. And we shall be faithful to this motto. The next step then is to draw the conclusions from this very simple sentence, conclusions that can be very painful and difficult.

One consequence, which is simple enough, concerns people of foreign origin who live amongst us. The African worker I see in the restaurant kitchen, this Moroccan I see digging a hole in the road, this veiled woman looking after children in a park: all these belong to the same world as me. That is the key point. That is where we reverse the dominant idea of the unity of the world in terms of objects, signs and elections, an idea that leads to persecution and war. The unity of the world is one of living and acting beings, here and now. And I must absolutely insist on this test of unity: these people who are here, different from me in terms of language, clothes, religion, food, education, exist in the same world, exist just as I myself do. Since they exist like me, I can converse with them, and then, as with anyone else, we can agree and disagree about things. But on the absolute precondition that they exist exactly as I do – in other words, in the same world.

This is the point at which the objection about cultural difference is raised. What do you mean? Are these people part of my world? Our world is made up of all those who genuinely accept 'our' values. For example, they are democrats, they respect women, they stand for human rights . . . Such people share the same world. But those with a different culture are not really part of our world. They are not democrats, they oppress women, they have barbaric customs . . . If they want to join our world, they have to learn our values; they have to share our values. The word used for all this is 'integration'; the person from elsewhere has to integrate into our world. In order for the world of the worker to be the same as ours, the masters of this world, he – the African worker – has to become the same as us. He has to love and practise the same values.

The current president of the French Republic, Nicolas Sarkozy, said at the time when he was both presidential candidate and in charge of the police: 'If foreigners want to remain in France, they have to love France; otherwise, they should leave.' And I told myself: I should leave, since I absolutely do not love the France of Nicolas Sarkozy; I do not share his values in the least. As against the prevailing opinion, I do not want anyone to be forced to leave, I am firmly against all expulsions. However, if someone absolutely had to be expelled I would much prefer it to be Sarkozy, for example, or the minister of expulsions Hortefeux,[2] rather than my African friends in the hostels. It is clear, in other words, that I'm not integrated. In reality, if you place conditions on the African worker belonging to the same world as you, you have already destroyed and abandoned this principle: 'There is only one world, that of living women and men.'

Philosophically, to say 'there is only one world' is to say that this world is precisely, in its very unity, a series of identities and differences. These differences, far from raising an objection to the unity of the world, are in fact its principle of existence. This is what I call the 'transcendental' of a world, that which gives it its immanent logical law.[3] 'Only one world' means that the transcendental measure of identificatory intensities, and thus of differences, is accessible everywhere to all, inasmuch as it is always the same. A unity such that, in order to have the right to figure in it, one had to be identical to all the elements that form part of it, would not be 'a world'. It would instead be a closed part of a world that overspills and erodes it. It would be –

2 [Brice Hortefeux is one of Nicolas Sarkozy's key political allies and since 2007 has been head of the newly named Ministry for Immigration, Integration and National Identity, thereby also becoming responsible for the deportation of illegal immigrants.]

3 The concept of the transcendental is developed at length and in technical detail in my last properly philosophical book, *Logique des mondes* (Paris: Seuil, 2006). See, in particular, the introduction to Book Two for an idea of the function of this concept, which is to govern the order of appearance of multiplicities in the world.

as if we wanted to return to what Fichte dreamed of under the name of the 'closed commercial state' – a return to the most barbaric forms of mental nationalism. Even common sense knows that everything is needed to make a world.

You might say that there are the laws of each country to take into account. Indeed. But a law is something completely different from a precondition. A law applies equally to all; it does not set a precondition for belonging to the world. It is simply a provisional rule that exists in a particular region of the single world. And no one is asked to love a law, simply to obey it.

The single world of living women and men may well have laws. What it cannot have is subjective or 'cultural' preconditions for existence within it. It cannot demand that, in order to live in it, you have to be like everyone else – still less, like a minority of these others, for example like the 'civilized' white petty bourgeois. If there is a single world, all those who live in it exist as much as I do, even though they are not like me, they are different. The single world is precisely the place where an unlimited set of differences exists. The world is transcendentally the same because the beings in this world are different.

If, on the contrary, those who live in the world are asked to be the same, this means that the world is closed in on itself and becomes, as a world, different from another world. Which inevitably sets the scene for separations, walls, controls, contempt, death, and finally war.

The question then arises whether anything governs these unlimited differences. Is there no identity that stands in a dialectical relationship with these differences? There may well be only one world, but does that mean that being French, or a Moroccan living in France, or Corsican, or

Breton, or Muslim in a country of Christian traditions, is nothing in the face of the immense differentiating unity of the world of living beings? We understand that the transcendental of the single world measures and governs differences. But should we then see the persistence of identities as an obstacle to the unity of the world? That is a good question. Certainly, the infinity of differences is also an infinity of identities. Let us examine more closely what the dialectic of identities involves when we maintain the existence of a single world in which a unique transcendental measures an infinity of differences.

First of all, what is an identity? The simplest definition is that an identity is the series of characteristics and properties by way of which an individual or a group recognizes itself as its 'self'. But what is this 'self'? It is what, across all the characteristic properties of identity, remains more or less invariable in the infinite web of differences and their changes. It is possible then to say that an identity is the abstract set of properties that support an invariance. For example, homosexual identity is composed of everything bound up with the invariance of the possible object of desire; the identity of an artist is that by which the invariance of his or her style can be recognized; the identity of a foreign community in a country is that by which membership of this can be recognized: language, gestures, dress, dietary habits, and so on.

Defined in this way by invariants, identity is doubly related to difference. First of all, identity is what is different from the rest – static identity. Second, identity is what does not become different – dynamic identity. In the background here, we have the great philosophical dialectic of Same and Other.

In accordance with the hypothesis that we are all living in a single world, it is possible to assert the right to be the same, to maintain and develop one's identity. If the Moroccan worker exists as I do, he can also assert that he has the right, just like me, to preserve and organize those invariant properties that are his: religion, mother tongue, forms of recreation and domesticity, and so on. He asserts his identity by refusing the imposition of integration, i.e. the pure and simple dissolution of his identity for the benefit of another. Because, if he exists in the world just as I do, he has no a priori reason to believe in this other identity any better than his own. That said, this assertion of identity has two quite different aspects, in the dialectic of same and other.

The first aspect is the desire that my becoming should remain within the same. A bit like Nietzsche's famous maxim: 'Become what you are.' It means the immanent development of identity in a new situation. The Moroccan worker does not abandon what it is that makes for his individual identity, whether in the family or society. But he gradually appropriates all this, in a creative fashion, wherever in the world he finds himself. He thus invents what he is: a Moroccan worker in Paris. We could say that he creates himself as a subjective movement, from the peasant of northern Morocco to the worker established in France. Without any internal breakage, but rather an expansion of identity.

The other way of asserting identity is negative. It consists in defending stubbornly that I am not the other. And this is often indispensable, for example when Sarkozy demands an authoritarian integration. The Moroccan worker forcibly asserts that his traditions and customs are not those of the petty-bourgeois European. He will even reinforce the characteristics of his religious or customary identity. He will oppose the Western world, refusing to accept its superiority.

There is finally in identity a double employment of difference. An assertive usage: the same maintains itself in its specific differentiating power. This is a creation. A negative usage: the same defends itself against its corruption by the other, and seeks to preserve its purity. All identity is the dialectical play of a movement of creation and a movement of purification. This dialectic creates, at different places in the world, shifts of identity and cancellations of difference, which make up the open history of the place itself.

To inscribe a politics of emancipation in the context of places – countries, for example – the best method is to assert first of all that there is only one world. And that the internal consequences of this axiom are inevitably political actions based on the indifference of differences, which means: politics is an operator for the consolidation of what is universal in identities. I can very precisely discuss with a Moroccan worker, or a housewife from Mali, what we can do together to assert that all of us exist in the same world, even if maintaining distinct identities.

For example, there was an appeal in France, launched by the L'Organisation politique and the Le rassemblement des collectifs des ouvriers sans papiers des foyers, to make 22 March 2007 a day of friendship with foreigners. 'Friendship' may have suspect connotations because it appeals to weakened forms of traditional humanism, but it is here a political word. A friend is quite simply someone who exists in equality with yourself, in the same world as you. That day, native French people and foreigners living here opened their identities to this movable dimension. They gathered to discuss their different ways of being in the same world. First of all, they together demanded the abolition of persecutory laws, laws that create walls, police raids and expulsions, laws that hand foreigners over to the police.[4] They demanded that the presence of millions of foreigners in France should be recognized simply in terms of their being here and existing like us. It is enough to note their existence in a friendly way and to regularize it, make it normal. To give them regular residence papers, on the basis of work, their children's education, severe illness impossible to treat in Africa, family demands or political risks. All things that are done very naturally for people who one knows are basically in the same existential situation as oneself. People of the same world.

In this collective trajectory, we make 'identities' a test-bed for political experience and its universality. As a perspective on the single world, identity becomes the support of what Maoists call an 'exchange of experiences'. The indigenous resident learns from the 'nomad' how the politics of our country is seen by people coming from elsewhere, and how they might envisage taking part in changing it; and the transitory or recent resident learns from the native French precisely how they have tried for a long time

4 A decisive point of action in France, as far as undocumented workers are concerned, is that of demanding without qualification the pure and simple abolition of the so-called CESEDA (Code de l'Entrée et du Séjour des Étrangers et du Droit d'Asile), a law cooked up by Sarkozy. This law is one of so many repressive and illegitimate laws initiated by Sarkozy and his henchman Brice Hortefeux, but it is particularly villainous. A detailed study of this infamous text was published as a supplement to *Journal politique*; this can be obtained from the address in Chapter 3, Note 1.

to change this kind of politics, and how they know that new arrivals have an essential part to play in the future of this struggle. Unpredictable new ideas result from this exchange, as well as forms of organization in which the difference between foreigners and nationals is no longer an operator of separation, because it is entirely subordinated to a common conviction: that there is a single world in which we exist on an equal basis, and that in this world, identities can constitute the material of a useful exchange of experiences, provided that we engage in common political action.

The train of thought developed above can be summed up as follows:

The 'world' of unleashed capitalism and the rich democracies is a false world. Recognizing only the unity of products and monetary signs, it casts the majority of humanity into the devalued world of the 'other', from which it separates itself by walls and war. In this sense, there is not a single world today.

To assert therefore that 'there is only one world' is a principle of action, a political imperative. This principle is also that of the equality of existences at every place in this single world.

The principle of the existence of a single world does not contradict the endless play of identities and differences. It simply means, when it becomes an axiom of collective action, that these identities subordinate their negative dimension (opposition to others) to their assertive dimension (development of the same).

As far as the existence of thousands of foreigners in our countries goes, there are three objectives: to oppose a persecutory integration; to limit communitarian closure and its nihilistic tendencies; and to develop the universal virtualities of identities. The concrete articulation of these three objectives defines what is most important in politics today.

On this intimate link between politics and the question of foreigners, so absolutely central today, there is an astonishing text of Plato's, at the end of Book Nine of *The Republic*. Socrates' young interlocutors say to him: 'What you tell us about politics is all well and good, but it is impossible. You cannot put it into practice.' And Socrates replies: 'Yes, in the city where we are born it is perhaps impossible. But perhaps it will possible in another city.' As if every genuine politics presupposes expatriation, exile, foreignness. We should remember this when we go and practise politics with foreign students, workers in the hostels, young people in the *banlieues*: Socrates is right, the fact that they are foreigners, or that their culture is different, is not an obstacle. On the contrary! The achievement of a genuine politics, at a place in this single world that we proclaim, absolutely does need those coming from elsewhere for its very possibility.

A Socialist prime minister said in the early 1980s, adopting the role of a 'civilized' mouthpiece for Le Pen: 'Immigrants are a problem.'[5] We must reverse this judgement and say: 'Foreigners are an opportunity!' The mass of foreign workers and their children bear witness, in our tired old countries, to the youth of the world, its widespread and its infinite variety. Without them we would sink into nihilistic consumption and an order imposed by the police.

5 [Probably a reference to Laurent Fabius, prime minister in the early 1980s, who notoriously claimed that the National Front raised the right questions (regarding immigration and so on), but offered the wrong solutions.]

Let foreigners teach us at least to become foreign to ourselves, to project ourselves sufficiently out of ourselves to no longer be captive to this long Western and white history that has come to an end, and from which nothing more can be expected than sterility and war. Against this catastrophic and nihilistic expectation of a security state, let us greet the foreignness of tomorrow.

5 Courage in these Circumstances

All the points that I listed above, and the dozens of others that you can invent for yourselves, bring us back to what I declared to be the crucial virtue of this time: courage. For the raising of impotence to impossibility is, subjectively, a question of courage. It means abandoning the rule of survival of the human animal, a poor thing today though elevated to a dizzy height under the name of 'individual', to hold on to a point that serves as a truth procedure.

There is a passage in Lacan's *Seminar: Book I* that I have always liked, in which he asks whether the analytic cure should not conclude with broad dialectical discussions on courage and justice – as in Plato's dialogues, he says. This reference to Plato, at the point of coming to the ultimate aims of the cure, is very striking. Courage is invoked in direct connection with the process of raising impotence to impossibility, which presupposes a redefinition of courage.

What then is courage? Read Plato's marvellous dialogue *Laches*, which is devoted precisely to this subject. The question is asked of a specialist, a general named Laches, who replies, in essence: 'Courage is when I see an enemy and run forward to fight him.' Socrates of course is not very convinced, and chides the general as follows: 'That is a fine example of courage, but an example is not a definition.' And the dialogue continues, tortuous as always, examining the very difficult notions of 'danger' and 'temerity', and succeeding only in eliminating false trails.

Running the same risks as General Laches, I shall give my own definition of courage. First of all, I want to preserve its status as a virtue. After all, what we are looking for is an ethic, a provisional ethic to avoid becoming either depressed or rats in Sarkozy's heavy weather. We want to know how to be dignified, virtuous, guardians of the future of truths, during this bad patch.

I define courage then as the virtue displayed by endurance in the impossible. It is not simply a question of encountering the impossible, experiencing it. For then we only have heroism, a moment of heroism. And, at the end of the day, heroism is easier than courage. Heroism is when one faces up to the impossible. It has always been represented as a posture, possibly a sublime one, because it is the moment at which one turns towards the impossible, in other words the Real that is required, and faces up to it. Courage is distinct from heroism because it is a virtue, and not a moment or a posture. It is a virtue to be constructed. For our part, as materialists of the event and the exception, we have to understand that a virtue is not something that one already has, a kind of disposition, which for example would divide people into the courageous and the cowardly. A virtue is displayed in practices that construct a particular time, regardless of the laws of the world or the opinions that support these laws. If heroism is the subjective figure of facing up to the impossible, then courage is the virtue of endurance in the impossible. Courage is not the point itself, it is holding on to this point. What demands courage is holding on, in a different duration from that imposed by the law of the world. The raw material of courage is time.

This can be said in a way that will seem particularly stupid: courage is not being too quickly discouraged. But this should rather be written 'dis-couraged', and we should understand courage as a virtue that is active exclusively in time: courage is 'couragement' that defeats dis-couragement. Our friends the African workers put this very clearly in their invented language, which is both rigorous and piquant. One of the aims of political work, they say, is to 'courage' people. But we must also recognize that, when the general situation is particularly bad, for example after the election of Sarkozy, many of those whom they know 'are not couraged'. They know that the virtue of courage lies in organized political action; it is not a state, but rather what takes hold of someone and vigorously 'courages' them. In other words, like any genuine virtue, courage is a verb rather than a noun.

After the election of Sarkozy, courage is required in order to escape from the impotence expressed in the affect of depression. But take care! Courage cannot be the courage to begin again, to reconstruct what used to be. The courage to continue to be 'couraged' is in no way reducible to the courage to preserve what was defeated. The 'reconstruction of the Left', the 'reform of the Socialist Party', is not our kind of thing! Nothing would be less likely to 'courage' us. Any repetition dis-courages.

On this point, we have to examine the dialectic of courage more closely. And recall first of all that the message of courage always brings with it a dose of heroism. We have first of all to turn towards a fixed point. We have to accept heroically to dissolve the individual into a face-to-face with the point to be held on to. And this is a heroic element. Not necessarily a grandiose heroism like that of the warrior (although sometimes that is also needed). But at the very minimum, we must turn towards the exceptional point and accept a move that removes us from the pressing interests of our individual animality. This turn by which the individual dis-individualizes is undoubtedly what Plato called 'conversion'. The dialectical conversion, as he understood it, removes us in fact from reality to bring us face to face with the Real, which Plato called 'Idea'. And this conversion, though entirely rational, is heroic in the sense that it is inscribed as a rupture in the fabric of the time of reality. In this sense, courage is never a virtue of re-establishment or repetition. Courage is never the courage to recommence as before.

Just after the election of the Rat Man, I was struck by the cover of the magazine *Marianne*, which declared, 'Don't Be Afraid!'[1] I found this very interesting. It is legitimate in its own way, accepting that fear is a generic element in the situation, and it seems to call for courage. But the content that *Marianne* gave to this courage was, as usual, only that of finally building a left, the true Left – that mythical creature. The repetitive and discouraging reasoning of *Marianne* is that we have, on the one hand, to liquidate libertarian ideas (meaning May '68, a point on which the 'republicans' of *Marianne* strikingly resemble the privileged classes who govern and their rats), and, on the other hand, not give up,

1 [Weekly news magazine of the 'republicanist' sensibility founded by Jean-François Kahn and Maurice Szafran in 1997 and well known for its splashy, not to say sensationalist, headlines.]

hold fast, keep working, rebuild! But this isn't courage. Courage doesn't mean to be stubbornly fixed on something, to keep on climbing the slope like Sisyphus. Courage, in the sense in which I understand it, has its origin in a heroic conversion, and is oriented towards a point that was not there, a Real woven out of the impossible. Courage starts at a point, a heroic turn that cuts through established opinions and does not tolerate any nostalgia, even if, in its essence, courage is the disciplined holding on to the consequences of the encounter with this point. Now, when something starts at such a point, we have to accept that it cannot immediately be measured against the overall situation. When you constitute a separate duration that starts at a point, you are not immediately placed in a confrontation between this localization and the global situation.

The blow received in the form of the election of Sarkozy is of a global character. It concerns the state, in other words what I call the state of the situation. It is sufficiently global that it may for a long while remain indistinct. We do not know yet which of its ingredients are the most significant, which are its priority localizations, how things will happen, and so on. There is simply a feeling being struck and of impotence. On the level of the situation taken globally, at the present time you have no possible way of curing this impotence. For the supposed global response, as we are only too familiar, is the old refrain of 'reconstruction of the Left'. This amounts to returning to the old ways, trying to patch up the burst tyre of the old parliamentary categories, and thus preparing without courage for another round of the same circumstances that create impotence.

We have here a major law of the provisional ethic: when you receive a global blow, the courage that responds to it is local. It is at one particular point that you are going to rebuild the possibility of living without losing your soul under the depressive effects of the blow received. Which leads us to a different definition of courage, or rather of the direction of its action: courage orients us locally amid the global disorientation.

The subjective situation of our country may be described as follows: the disorientation of minds, the factor of impotence, has been under way for a long while, at least since Mitterrand, who was a cunning organizer of confusion. But with the election of Sarkozy, the rallying of the rats and universal inertia, it has finally found its symbol, the forms of rupture that now constitute the law of the situation. In these conditions, the imperative is to orient ourselves locally, point by point, in such a way as to reconstitute courage.

In circumstances such as these, local courage makes a breach in a global disposition of which Sarkozy is the name, the name of the state. But what is this breach?

6 France's Transcendental: Pétainism

We are looking for an analytical element bearing on the particular nature of the disorientation of minds that goes by the name of Sarkozy. I would like to take up in greater detail at this point a hypothesis already presented: that to grasp this disorientation in its overall dimension, its historicity and intelligibility, we need to go back to what should be called its Pétainist transcendental.

Let us make clear the intellectual nature of this hypothesis. I am not saying that circumstances today resemble the defeat of 1940, or that Sarkozy resembles Pétain. Not at all. I am saying that the mass subjectivity that brought Sarkozy to power, and sustains his actions, finds its unconscious national-historical roots in Pétainism. This is what I call a transcendental: something that, without appearing on the surface – so that our situation does not 'resemble' the sequence of Pétain's reign – configures from afar, gives law and order, to a collective mechanism. I have already used this idea (see Chapter 3, Note 1) to clarify what should be understood by the prescriptive statement 'There is only one world.'

In the case of our country, to call this transcendental 'Pétainist' avoids describing it weakly as anti-democratic or Bonapartist, which are standard terms of the 'leftist' vocabulary, or describing it as fascist or pre-fascist, which would be excessive, ultra-left.

I propose to say that 'Pétainism' is the transcendental, in France, of catastrophic forms of disorientation taken by the state. We have a major disorientation, this is presented as a turning point in the situation, and is solemnly active at the head of the state. From this point of view, still a formal one, there is a national tradition of Pétainism that goes back well beyond Pétain himself. Pétainism in France actually goes back to the Restoration of 1815. A post-revolutionary government was re-established in the foreigners' baggage-train, with the vigorous backing of émigrés, overthrown classes, traitors and opportunists of all kinds, and the consent of a worn-out population. It declared that it would restore public order and morals after the bloody anarchy of revolution. This matrix, a typically French one, is persistent in our history. In 1940, we find the catastrophic figure of military defeat as the pretext for a major disorientation: so that, for example, a government that spoke incessantly of the 'nation' was installed by foreigners; oligarchs corrupt to the marrow presented themselves as fit to lead the country out of a great moral crisis; an adventurer, a doddery old man, retired soldier and wily politician always at the service of the most wealthy, presented himself as the genuine upholder of the nation's energy.

Are there not many characteristics of this kind today, in a wretched repetition of these severe historical depressions that France has inflicted on itself?

First of all, in this kind of 'Pétainist' situation, capitulation and servility present themselves as invention, revolution and regeneration. It was absolutely essential for Sarkozy to campaign on the theme of a 'rupture'. Rupture, deep reforms, a ceaseless, mosquito-like movement: Sarkozy proclaims he will overcome the moral crisis of France, he will put the country back to work. It's no small thing to tell people, given the shape they're in, and in his three-piece suit as mayor of Neuilly: 'I shall put you back to work!' – rather like a nineteenth-century bourgeois lady addressing her maid. But no, it's rupture and renovation. The real content of course is unconditional obedience to the potentates of world capitalism. Military matters are the Americans' business, the domestic situation the business of the big financiers, and so on. It's only the weak, the poor, the foreigners who will be hit. This 'rupture' is in reality a politics of uninterrupted bowing and scraping that presents itself as a politics of national regeneration. This is a typically Pétainist disorientation: the leader called his servility towards the powers that be – the Nazi conquerors and their far-right accomplices – a 'national revolution'! At the nadir of capitulation and accepted servitude, the talk was of moral revival and a regenerated future. You'd have to go a long way to find anything more disorientating. It is a figure, I believe, that is characteristic of France, inasmuch as I don't find any ready equivalent in other nations, at least among those that claim a major role on the world stage, which France evidently did in the 1940s. This singularity is certainly no occasion for patriotic pride . . .

The second criterion of Pétainism is the theme of 'crisis', 'moral crisis', which justifies the measures taken in the name of regeneration. There is a national debasement, a threatening decadence, which has to be remedied immediately.

This debasement – today the preferred word is 'decline' – is attributed to a moral crisis; a crisis of discernment between right and wrong, of work, family and country. Because the crisis is a moral one, correction in no way requires a political mobilization of the people, something that indeed has to be prevented as effectively as possible, with draconian police measures. Morality comes in here, as it always does, in place of politics and against it, and especially against any politics directly inspired by the common people. Appeal is made to moral correction, work, the household economy, a precisely Pétainist terminology, which makes it possible to say that the state must be responsible for everything, since people are in a state of moral crisis. In the darkness of this crisis, only those individuals should be honoured who make meritorious efforts against decline at the appeal of the state and its leader. For example, by rejoicing in working sixty hours a week. People like this are given chocolate medals. As the Rat Man constantly repeats, 'Merit should be rewarded'.

This typically Pétainist dialectic of morality and politics, we may say, has been long prepared by all those who, from the 'new philosophers' of the late 1970s onwards, have 'moralized' historical judgement and substituted, for the fundamental opposition between the politics of egalitarian emancipation and the politics of inegalitarian conservation, a purely moral opposition between despotic and cruel states and states based on law – without of course explaining the origin of the gigantic massacres committed on a planetary scale for a century and a half by these 'lawful' states. The object of this moralization is in reality a political one. The point is to maintain that the state of the country is in no way the result of the action of the high servants of capital and their clientele in the media and in politics, but rather the fault of the people, the 'morality' of certain citizens. Sarkozy explains to us that, if our fellow citizens are plunged in a moral crisis that is leading the country to decline, this is – as you might suspect – because of May '68. Now May '68 was of course the work of the people, the young students, the workers, the intellectuals. And if May '68 still haunts Sarkozy and his rats, it is because they suppose, and not without reason, that people still continue more or less to believe in it, or to refer to it. This is why it is the people, and particularly young people from the *banlieues* and workers of foreign origin, who according to the Rat Man are the agents of a serious moral crisis. It is the fault of these thread-bare scum that the country is on the decline, that it is sinking from one moment to the next. Fortunately, Sarkozy and the state are vigilant. They will take responsibility for the whole operation of regeneration and rupture. The 'moral crisis' is always a proclamation aiming to give full powers to the state, on the pretext of the irresponsibility of the governed, and particularly of the most deprived and weak. How a moral crisis is to be repaired by state action is certainly not very clear. What is clear, however, is that energetic measures must be taken, and they certainly will be. That is what all the moralizing hotchpotch boils down to: police, justice, control, expulsions, villainous laws and prison system. Along with the enrichment of the rich, of course, which is the Good *par excellence*.

A third criterion of Pétainism is the paradigmatic function of foreign experience. The example of correction always comes from abroad. Foreigners do it better than we do, they have already been correcting for a long time, and over-come their moral crises without showing weakness. In the 'good' foreign countries, the demoralizers have been shown what for! It's up to us to follow suit at last. For Pétain, the good foreigners were the ones who radically clamped down on those responsible for moral crisis and decadence – Jews, Communists, half-castes, progressive intellectuals, and the like. It was the Fascists – Mussolini's Italy, Hitler's Germany, and Franco's Spain – who had put their countries back on their feet, and we had to do the same, after the example of those great models. It is quite obsessive, this reference to correction abroad as a matrix for correction here. There is a political aesthetic at work here, a theory of model and imitation. Like Plato's demiurge, the state had to shape society with its eyes fixed on the fascist models, if it was to pull it out of this terrible moral crisis. The advantage, for the rescuing state and its indefatigable leader, of this theory or aesthetic of the model – a subject on which Lacoue-Labarthe has written a remarkable essay[1] – quite wretched versions of which we face today, is that it involves a passive reconfiguration, which in no way summons the energy of its actors. This is precisely the role of the constant invocation, by our new reactionaries, of the remarkable merits of the American economy and universities under Bush, the magnificent reforms of Blair, or even the abnegation of the Chinese workers, who work twelve hours a day for practically nothing. 'One more effort, Frenchmen, if you wish to be modern like our neighbours and rivals.' The foreign model signifies that the only way out of the 'moral crisis' is through powerful new means of policing and

1 Philippe Lacoue-Labarthe died a few months ago, and his absence is cruelly felt in these difficult times. His *L'Imitation des modernes* (Paris: Galilée, 1986), well worth rereading, is an admirable book in which the ideological function of models and their reproduction is analysed in detail, in its operation as a suture, always pre-fascist, between politics and art.

repression, severe restrictions on the right to strike, cutbacks in public expenditure, and other fixtures of the friends of order, to make the mass of ordinary people sweat a bit. Only then, with the rich as rich as they can be, and the poor having been further impoverished, will we be able to celebrate the return of public morality.

A fourth and very important characteristic of the Pétainist mechanism is propaganda that maintains that some time ago something damaging happened to crystallize and aggravate the moral crisis. This is a key point. Pétainist propaganda largely consists in saying that the origin of moral crisis and decline lies in a disastrous event, always bound up with popular demands. With the proto-Pétainists of the Restoration in 1815, this was of course the Revolution, the Terror, the beheading of the king. With the Pétainism of Pétain himself, the disaster was the Popular Front. This was just four years after the Léon Blum government and, above all, the great strikes and factory occupations. These unspeakable disorders had aroused a memorable fear among the possessing classes, from which they were still trembling. They far preferred the Germans, the Nazis, no matter whom, to the Popular Front. Hence the proposition that the Popular Front was the origin and symbol of the grave moral crisis that required a national revolution – with the welcome support of the Nazi occupier. For our president today, May '68 was responsible for a crisis of values, which equally necessitates a reconfiguration of our entire unhappy country, well advanced on accelerating disintegration, after the model of Bush or Blair. There is a historical element in Pétainism that consists in linking two events: a negative event, generally with a working-class and popular structure, and a positive event, with a state, electoral and/or military structure. One of the strengths of Pétainism is that it proposes a simplified reading of history. For Sarkozy, this reading covers a fairly large arc, forty years of history from the nadir of decadence, May '68, to the apogee of correction, the Rat Man in person. This is a source of legitimacy for the new government, since all legitimacy of this kind is a link between the state and history. The government represents itself, and has itself represented, as a historical actor of the first importance, since it is this government that has finally embarked on the correction needed in the wake of the inaugural damaging event.

The fifth element is racist. Under Pétain this was quite explicit: get rid of the Jews, the half-castes, the blacks . . . Today this is voiced in a more subtle fashion, but an attentive ear can still hear it: 'We are not an inferior race' – the implication being 'contrary to others'. 'France does not have to take lessons from anyone, everything that France has done has always been right, and true French people do not have to doubt the legitimacy of their country's actions.' Sarkozy has already gone a long way in this direction, not hesitating to compare us very favourably with the Africans. He has let them know that they are far from being as deserving as us, and that consequently, if they are in a sorry state in their countries, it is their own fault and they have to stay there. We, the native French, have our own tasks, our own values, our own destiny, our own existence, and it is to these that we shall devote our efforts. Of course, we need labourers, road-sweepers, refuse collectors . . . These can be hand-picked, and are requested not to make a fuss or complain about their evident inferiority, poorly integrated as they are. As with Pétain himself, there is an intellectual clique ready to applaud the Rat Man's racist blustering.

Let us summarize the five formal characteristics that define the Pétainist transcendental. First of all, the disorientation created by an explicit reversal of the real content of state action: talk of revolution when there is black reaction, of regeneration when there is capitulation, of a new freedom when there is complete servility. Second, the anti-political theme of moral crisis, which blames the people and gives the state a free hand to organize new forms of repression. Third, the theme of a harmful event as the origin and symbol of moral decline, an event that is always a striking episode in the political advance of the working class and people – the Revolution under Robespierre, the Commune, the Popular Front, May '68. Fourth, the paradigmatic function and value of the model of correction, of the most striking forms of extreme reaction to the foreigner. Fifth, the numerous variants relating the superiority of our civilization both to foreign populations – Africans, for example – and to internal 'minorities' such as young Arabs.

In the light of these criteria, we can say without hesitation that Sarkozy falls under the Pétainist transcendental.

7   The Incorruptible

What is the scenario of this 'soft' Pétainism? It starts with reinforcing the protection of fortunes and their transmission by inheritance: suppression of inheritance tax, less or even no tax on very high incomes and properties, encouragement for speculation of all kinds. After some summer entertainment and sleight of hand to distract the remains of the Left, an insidious and ferocious war is launched against the people, and particularly against those families and individuals who are most exposed. The people are supposed to remain calm, in their place. And everyone deserves the place that they have. The apology for merit means this and nothing else: everyone simply has what they deserve, and if they find themselves at the bottom of a hole, then they deserve to be there. And all this with a great deal of police deployment at home, and obscure negotiations, dodgy transactions and military operations abroad.

The constant resort to 'business', secret diplomacy and crooked deals, as well as the ostentatious display of the power of money, the potentially limitless universe opened by wealth, all this makes up one of the most striking features of Sarkozy:

he visibly thinks that the whole world is corruptible. The moment has come, and he claims the glory for this, to show that corruption is not a marginal vice, but lies at the heart of our universe. To buy, to be bought, emoluments, positions, yachts, luxury gifts – what's wrong with any of this? With Sarkozy a new page opens in the ties between politics and corruption: the eradication of any idea that one can be – as Robespierre was nicknamed – 'Incorruptible'. But what kind of corruption are we talking about here?

Corruption is a classic theme of anti-parliamentary propaganda, particularly that of the far right: the Panama scandal and the Stavisky Affair under the Third Republic, the Indochina currency scandal under the Fourth Republic, and – under the Fifth Republic – Bernard Tapie, Michel Noir, Roland Dumas and so many others, including, perhaps, Chirac in person.[2] 'They're all on the take' is the summary verdict on the typical media presentation of the links between money and politicians. Of course it is in a very different register that I shall speak of corruption, or indeed that Robespierre did. It is likewise in a different register that a lasting impression is left on public opinion, even at the electoral level. Of all the mayors, regional councillors and various notables who, despite being accused or suspected of corruption in this narrow sense, have been triumphantly re-elected, the Balkany couple are the canonical example.[3] In 2002, it was tempting to contrast the virtuous

2 This section on the essence of corruption under representative regimes develops an article that *Le Nouvel Observateur* commissioned but did not publish.

3 [Patrick Balkany, centre-right politician, mayor of Levallois-Perret – in the upper-class northwestern suburbs of Paris – from 1983 to 1995 and again since 2001, and parliamentary representative for Hauts-de-Seine from 1988 to 1997 and again since 2002. Together with his wife Isabelle, he was found guilty several times for the embezzlement of public funds, to a total estimated between one and five million euros, through various schemes such as the invention of fake jobs for public employees.]

Jospin to the (supposedly) corrupt Chirac. But neither the praise nor the indignation that resulted prevented them from being equally discomfited in the first round of the presidential election. We have to look rather further back than this. And rather higher, as well.

We are in 1793, with the Revolution under desperate attack. Saint-Just asks, 'What do they want who accept neither Terror nor Virtue?' An intimidating question, to which the practice of the Thermidorians gave a clear response: they wanted a certain degree of corruption to be accepted as normal. Instead of the Revolutionary dictatorship, they wanted 'freedom', by which they meant the right to do business, and mix their own business with that of the state. They equally opposed both the 'terrorist' and 'liberticidal' repression of dodgy deals, and the virtuous obligation to consider only the public good. Montesquieu had already noted that democracy, by granting everyone a fragment of power, was prey to a permanent confusion between private interests and the public good. He made virtue into an obligatory disposition of governments of this type. Mandated without any other guarantee than the suffrage, those who govern must in a certain sense forget themselves and repress their own tendencies to exercise power simply as a function of personal enjoyment, or the enjoyment of the dominant milieus (the rich, as a general rule).

The idea goes back to Plato. In his radical critique of the democratic regime, Plato noted how, from the standpoint of such a regime, what politics has to regulate is the anarchy of material desires. And as a consequence of this, a democratic government is unsuited to the service of any true idea at all, since if the public power is in the service of desires and their satisfaction, which ultimately means in the service of the economy in the broad sense of the term, then it obeys only two criteria: wealth, which gives the most stable abstract means for this satisfaction, and opinion, which determines the objects of desire and the inner force with which people believe it necessary to appropriate these.

The French revolutionaries, who were republicans and not democrats, termed 'corruption' the subjection of governmental power to business matters. We are today so persuaded that the chief objectives of government are indeed economic growth, the standard of living, the abundance of commodities, the upward movement of share prices, the growth of capital and the eternal prosperity of the rich, that it is hard for us to understand what the revolutionaries understood by 'corruption'. It was not so much the fact that any particular individuals enriched themselves by profiting from their position of power, but rather the general idea, the work of opinion, that consists in holding that enrichment, whether collective or private, is the natural goal of political action. 'Corruption' in this sense is essentially expressed in Guizot's famous slogan: 'Enrich yourselves!'

But do we have a different slogan today? Doesn't everyone accept that it is the state of the economy that determines the electoral mood, so that everything simply hinges on the ability to make at least the average citizen believe that things are going to be better for business, great and small, if they vote the right way? And that politics is therefore never more than a matter of its subjects' self-interest?

Corruption, from this point of view, is not something that threatens the functioning of democracy. It is its genuine essence. Whether politicians are personally corrupt or not in the everyday sense of the word has almost no bearing at all on this essential corruption. At that level, Jospin and Chirac are birds of a feather.

Marx remarked, at the very beginnings of representative democracy in Europe, that the governments appointed by universal suffrage were simply foundations for the power of Capital. They are still more so today than they were then! For if democracy means representation, it is first of all the representation of the general system that bears its forms. In other words: electoral democracy is only representative in so far as it is first of all the consensual representation of capitalism, or of what today has been renamed the 'market economy'. This is its underlying corruption, and it is no trivial matter that the great humanist thinker Marx, that Enlightenment philosopher, believed it necessary to oppose to such a 'democracy' a transitional dictatorship, which he called the dictatorship of the proletariat. A strong term, 'dictatorship', but it illuminates the twists and turns of the dialectic between representation and corruption.

What poses a problem is really the definition of democracy. As long as we are persuaded, like the Thermidorians and their liberal descendants, that it resides in the free play of interests of particular groups or individuals, we shall see it deteriorate, slowly or rapidly according to circumstances, into a hopeless corruption. Genuine democracy, which is what I believe we have to preserve, is a quite different concept.[4] It is equality in the face of the Idea, the political

---

4 I do indeed maintain that we have to preserve a positive use of the word 'democracy', rather than abandon it entirely to its prostitution by capitalo-parliamentarism. I have explained this point in a chapter of my book *Metapolitics* (London: Verso, 2005). In a general sense, I prefer the struggle for a reappropriation of names to the pure and simple creation of new names, even if the latter is often required. That is why I also preserve without hesitation, and despite the sombre experiences of the last century, the fine word 'communism'.

Idea. For a long time, for example, this meant the revolutionary or communist Idea. It is the ruin of this Idea that identifies 'democracy' with general corruption.

The enemy of democracy has not been so much the despotism of the single party (misnamed 'totalitarianism'), but rather the fact that this despotism brought to an end the first sequence of the communist Idea. The only real question is how to open a second sequence of this Idea, and make it prevail over the play of interests by other means than bureaucratic terrorism. A new definition, in other words, and a new practice, of what was called 'dictatorship' (of the proletariat). Or again, what comes to the same thing, a new use of the word 'virtue'.

This is not – yet – the path that most clearly lies open before us. With Sarkozy, the necessity of corruption in its intellectual sense, in other words the harmony that is supposed to exist between private interests and the public good, need no longer be concealed, and seeks even to be openly displayed. We are far now from Mitterrand, who, while actually full of indulgence towards corruption, and well aware that it was necessary in the world that we have, still advised Bernard Tapie to distrust it, saying that 'the French do not love money'.[5] The main battle of our great Sarkozy is to insist that we can, and should, love money. We should stop seeing this love as a shameful secret and should repress once again the unfortunate association of money with excrement so perceptively uncovered by Freud. The famous case of the Rat Man, as you can read in Freud's 'Notes Upon a Case of Obsessional Neurosis', was also an anal business.

5 [French businessman associated with the Socialist Party and now with the Radical Party, who became a symbol in the 1980s of the corruption scandals that engulfed the political establishment.]

'In such great misfortune, what remains to you?' Corneille's Medea is asked by her confidante; to which she replies with the magnificent words, 'Myself! Myself, I say, and it's enough!' She still has the courage to decide on her own existence. I therefore propose the following idea: if 'Pétainism' stands for the transcendental of possible abjections of our country, the logical invariant of its corruption, then all courage is the courage not to be Pétainist. This is the narrowest definition. After all, it defines the courage of the Resistance in the strict sense, before 1944 in any case. The choice of joining the Resistance was the choice of the real point that courage had to hold on to, in an element that was a complete opposition to Pétainism. It was not enough to be against Nazism and the occupation in order to join the Resistance. What was needed was a disgust towards Pétainism, that specifically French infection of subjectivity.

We should note, however, that Pétainism can in no way be reduced simply to the leading personnel of collaboration between 1940 and 1944. As you can see by the definitions I have given, Pétainism is a mass subjective form. If we want to define in a positive way what it is that withstands passive contagion by this form, it is not enough to see the Resistance purely as the opposition to Nazism and Pétainist complicity; we should rather define it affirmatively in terms of its courage in holding on to a point absolutely at variance with what Pétainism represented. And this is indeed the maxim that I have proposed to you in the context of the election of Sarkozy.

To support this tension, it is useful to explicitly contradict the Pétainist doctrine of the unhappy event that they declare to be the origin of present decadence: the Popular Front for Pétain himself, May '68 for Sarkozy. Anyone who holds on to a point heterogeneous to the Pétainist consensus must dispose, by way of a personal allegory, of a public appeal to happy events. It is important that the subjective immanence is not the aggressive, gloomy, policing kind that claims to repair the consequences of an unhappy event, but rather one that asserts itself as creatively faithful to some happy event in personal or political life. A raging love affair, for example, or the destruction of slavery by the black insurrection in Haiti in 1793, or the initial emotion provided by the luminous demonstration, finally grasped, of a very hard mathematical theorem. Or the overwhelming contemplation of an abstract painting. Or May '68, of course. Our own task is one that I like to call 'resistance', given that the maxim of its courage and the emblematic events it appeals to are affirmative.

Those who fly a half-mast flag of decadence, and present themselves as able to restore lost glories, should always be distrusted. Their intentions are not pure. Anyone who really does claim to be on the side of creation, affirmation and an egalitarian collective future – the side of truths, in other words – must rather appeal to those truths that already (and as if in the intemporal neighbourhood of what is being proposed) give us the pleasure of appearing at a particular place, in the singular force of their universality.

We should also understand that salvation never comes from the imitation of an external model. We whose flags are decorated with allegories of the happy element are pleased if anyone else who escapes the Pétainist consensus takes them over. It was one of the most depressing aspects of the last electoral campaign that both protagonists appealed to Blair. There is a Chinese expression that I rather like that describes two accomplices who are up to no good. The Chinese say, 'Yes, those two are badgers from the same hillside.' And indeed, Royal and Sarkozy, like Blair and Bush, were indeed badgers – *blaireaux* – from the same hillside.

Negatively, we need only say: neither rat, nor *blaireau*.

8 Must the Communist Hypothesis Be Abandoned?

I would like to situate the Sarkozy episode, which is not an impressive page in French history, in a broader horizon.[1] Let us picture a kind of Hegelian fresco of recent world history – by which I do not, like our journalists, mean the triad Mitterrand–Chirac–Sarkozy, but rather the development of the politics of working-class and popular emancipation over nearly two centuries.

Since the French Revolution and its gradually universal echo, since the most radically egalitarian developments of that revolution, the decrees of Robespierre's Committee of Public Safety on the 'maximum' and Babeuf's theorizations, we know (when I say 'we', I mean humanity in the abstract, and the knowledge in question is universally available on the paths of emancipation) that *communism is the right hypothesis*. Indeed, there is no other, or at least I am not aware of one. All those who abandon this hypothesis

---

1 This discussion of the communist hypothesis was presented on 13 June 2007 at my monthly seminar held at the École Normale Supérieure (see Chapter 1, Note 1).

immediately resign themselves to the market economy, to parliamentary democracy – the form of state suited to capitalism – and to the inevitable and 'natural' character of the most monstrous inequalities.

What do we mean by 'communism'? As Marx argued in the *1844 Manuscripts*, communism is an idea regarding the destiny of the human species. This use of the word must be completely distinguished from the meaning of the adjective 'communist' that is so worn-out today, in such expressions as 'communist parties', 'communist states' or 'communist world' – never mind that 'communist state' is an oxymoron, to which the obscure coinage 'socialist state' has wisely been preferred. Even if, as we shall see, these uses of the word belong to a time when the hypothesis was still coming-to-be.

In its generic sense, 'communist' means first of all, in a negative sense – as we can read in its canonical text *The Communist Manifesto* – that the logic of classes, of the fundamental subordination of people who actually work for a dominant class, can be overcome. This arrangement, which has been that of history ever since antiquity, is not inevitable. Consequently, the oligarchic power of those who possess wealth and organize its circulation, crystallized in the might of states, is not inescapable. The communist hypothesis is that a different collective organization is practicable, one that will eliminate the inequality of wealth and even the division of labour: every individual will be a 'multi-purpose worker', and in particular people will circulate between manual and intellectual work, as well as between town and country. The private appropriation of monstrous fortunes and their transmission by inheritance will disappear. The existence of a coercive state separate from civil society, with its military and police, will no longer seem a self-evident necessity. There will be, Marx tells us – and he saw this point as his major contribution – after a brief sequence of 'proletarian dictatorship' charged with destroying the remains of the old world, a long sequence of reorganization on the basis of a 'free association' of producers and creators, which will make possible a 'withering away' of the state.

'Communism' as such only denotes this very general set of intellectual representations. This set is the horizon of any initiative, however local and limited in time it may be, that breaks with the order of established opinions – the necessity of inequalities and the state instrument for protecting these – and composes a fragment of a politics of emancipation. In other words, communism is what Kant called an 'Idea', with a regulatory function, rather than a programme. It is absurd to characterize communist principles in the sense I have defined them here as utopian, as is so often done. They are intellectual patterns, always actualized in a different fashion, that serve to produce lines of demarcation between different forms of politics. By and large, a particular political sequence is either compatible with these principles or opposed to them, in which case it is reactionary. 'Communism', in this sense, is a heuristic hypothesis that is very frequently used in political argument, even if the word itself does not appear. If it is still true, as Sartre said, that 'every anti-communist is a swine', it is because any political sequence that, in its principles or lack of them, stands in formal contradiction with the communist hypothesis in its generic sense, has to be judged as opposed to the emancipation of the whole of humanity, and thus to the properly human destiny of humanity. Whoever does not illuminate the coming-to-be of humanity with the communist hypothesis – whatever words they use, as such words matter little – reduces humanity, as far as its collective becoming is concerned, to animality. As we know, the contemporary – that is, the capitalist name of this animality – is 'competition'. The war dictated by self-interest, and nothing more.

As a pure Idea of equality, the communist hypothesis has no doubt existed in a practical state since the beginnings of the existence of the state. As soon as mass action opposes state coercion in the name of egalitarian justice, we have the appearance of rudiments or fragments of the communist hypothesis. This is why, in a pamphlet titled *De l'idéologie*, which I wrote in collaboration with the late lamented François Balmès and was published in 1976, we proposed to identify 'communist invariants'.[2] Popular revolts, such as that of the slaves led by Spartacus, or that of the German peasants led by Thomas Münzer, are examples of this practical existence of communist invariants.

However, in the explicit form that it was given by certain thinkers and activists of the French Revolution, the communist hypothesis inaugurates political modernity. It was this that laid low the mental structures of the *ancien régime*, yet without being tied to those 'democratic' political forms that the bourgeoisie would make the instrument for its own pursuit of power. This point is essential: from the beginning, the communist hypothesis in no way coincided with the 'democratic' hypothesis that would lead to present-day

2 [*De l'idéologie* was published by Éditions Maspero in the Collection Yenan, Série Synthèses.]

parliamentarism. It subsumes a different history and different events. What seems important and creative when illuminated by the communist hypothesis is different in kind from what bourgeois-democratic historiography selects. That is indeed why Marx, giving materialist foundations to the first effective great sequence of the modern politics of emancipation, both took over the word 'communism' and distanced himself from any kind of democratic 'politicism' by maintaining, after the lesson of the Paris Commune, that the bourgeois state, no matter how democratic, must be destroyed.

Well, I leave it to you to judge what is important or not, to judge the points whose consequences you choose to assume against the horizon of the communist hypothesis. Once again, it is the right hypothesis, and we can appeal to its principles, whatever the declensions or variations that these undergo in different contexts.

Sartre said in an interview, which I paraphrase: If the communist hypothesis is not right, if it is not practicable, well, that means that humanity is not a thing in itself, not very different from ants or termites. What did he mean by that? If competition, the 'free market', the sum of little pleasures, and the walls that protect you from the desire of the weak, are the alpha and omega of all collective and private existence, then the human animal is not worth a cent.

And it is this worthlessness to which Bush with his aggressive conservatism and crusader spirit, Blair the Pious with his militarist rhetoric, and Sarkozy with his 'work, family, country' discipline, want to reduce the existence of the immense majority of living individuals. And the 'Left' is still worse, simply juxtaposing to this vacant violence a vague spirit of charity. To morbid competition, the pasteboard victories of daddy's boys and girls, the ridiculous supermen of unleashed finance, the coked-up heroes of the planetary stock exchange, this Left can only oppose the same actors with a bit of social politeness, a little walnut oil in the wheels, crumbs of holy wafer for the disinherited – in other words, borrowing from Nietzsche, the bloodless figure of the 'last man'.

To put an end once and for all to May '68 means agreeing that our only choice is between the hereditary nihilism of finance and social piety. It not only means accepting that communism collapsed in the Soviet Union, not only acknowledging that the Parti Communiste Français has been wretchedly defeated, but also and above all it means abandoning the hypothesis that May '68 was a militant invention precisely aware of the failure of state 'communism'. And thus that May '68, and still more so the five years that followed, inaugurated a new sequence for the genuine communist hypothesis, one that always keeps its distance from the state. Certainly, no one could say where all this might lead, but we knew in any case that what was at stake was the rebirth of this hypothesis.

If the thing that Sarkozy is the name of succeeds in imposing the necessity of abandoning any idea of a rebirth of this kind, if human society is a collection of individuals pursuing their self-interest, if this is the eternal reality, then it is certain that the philosopher can and must abandon the human animal to its sad destiny.

But we shall not let a triumphant Sarkozy dictate the meaning of our existence, or the tasks of philosophy. For what we are witnessing in no way imposes such a renunciation of the communist hypothesis, but simply a consideration of the moment at which we find ourselves in the history of this hypothesis.

9 The History of the Communist Hypothesis and Its Present Moment

We need a historical fresco on which to situate our efforts. There have been two great sequences in the communist hypothesis: that of its setting up, its installation, and that of the first attempt at its realization.

The first sequence runs from the French Revolution to the Paris Commune, say from 1792 to 1871. It thus lasted nearly eighty years. This sequence introduced all kinds of entirely new political phenomena into a wide range of countries across the world. And yet we can say that, as far as its major trajectory was concerned, it was essentially French. Marx himself, though he assigned the philosophical foundation of the sequence to Germany (the Hegelian dialectic), and its scientific turn to England (the birth of political economy), assigned its actual political content, in the order of practice, to France (the French workers' movement).[1]

1 For the function of the 'French workers' movement' in the genesis of Marxism, parallel to that of 'German philosophy' and 'English political economy', see Lenin's very fine text 'The Three Sources and Three Component Parts of Marxism', in Volume 19 of his *Collected Works* and available at: <http://www.marxists.org/archive/lenin/works/1913/mar/x01.htm>.

This sequence combined, under the sign of communism, the mass popular movement and a thematic of the seizure of power. The object was to organize the popular movement, in multiple forms – demonstrations, strikes, uprisings, armed actions, and so on – in preparation for an overturn, evidently meaning an insurrectional overturn such as went by the name of 'revolution'. This revolution would suppress the form of society (private property, inheritance, the division of humanity into nations, the division of labour, and so on) and establish communist equality, or what those working-class thinkers analysed so well by Jacques Rancière called the 'community of Equals'.[2]

The old order would be defeated by a combination of its own immanent corruption, and the pressure, possibly armed, of the popular movement. This was also the moment when the particular parameter of the workers' movement appeared. The old revolutionary categories – the common people of the towns, the artisans, students and intellectuals, the poor peasant masses – were transformed and relieved by the leading function of the working class.

This sequence was closed by the striking novelty and radical defeat of the Paris Commune. The Commune was the supreme form of this combination of popular movement, working-class leadership and armed insurrection. It showed the extraordinary vitality of this formula: it was able to exercise a new type of power for two months, in one of the great capital cities of Europe, with the internal support of

2 On the nineteenth-century origin of the figure of the worker as political and ideological reference, its consequences in the field of thought, and the doctrine of the 'community of Equals' that is linked with it, it is clearly necessary to read the great works of Jacques Rancière, and in particular his two very fine books *The Nights of Labour* (Philadelphia: Temple University Press, 1991) and *The Ignorant Schoolmaster* (Palo Alto: Stanford University Press, 1991).

many foreign revolutionaries, particularly Poles, which showed the strength of the Marxist concept of the International. But it equally showed the limits of the formula. For it was unable to give the revolution a national scope, or to organize effective resistance when the counter-revolution, with the tacit support of foreign powers, succeeded in bringing to bear a competent military response.

The second sequence ran from 1917 (the Russian Revolution) to 1976 (the end of the Cultural Revolution in China, but also the end of the militant movement that arose throughout the world around the years 1966–76, and the epicentre of which, from the point of view of political novelty, was May 1968 in France and its consequences in the years that followed). This second sequence ran for just over half a century. We should also note, however, that it was divided from the first by a break of nearly the same length (more than forty years).

This second sequence, which was very complex, and of whose final stage we ourselves are the heirs, was dominated by the question of time. How to achieve victory? How, as against the Paris Commune, to endure in the face of the bloody reaction of the possessors and their mercenaries? How to organize the new power, the new state, in such a way as to protect it from destruction by its enemies? Lenin's great question was to answer these questions. And it was not for nothing that he danced in the snow when the insurrectionary power in Russia had lasted a day longer than the Paris Commune.

During this second sequence, the problem was no longer the existence of a popular working-class movement acting on the basis of the communist hypothesis, nor was it the generic idea of revolution in its insurrectionary form. The problem was that of victory and duration. We can say that it was no longer a question of formulating the communist hypothesis and experimenting with it, but rather of realizing it. From this point of view, Lenin formulated the general maxim more or less as follows: 'We are entering the period of victorious proletarian revolutions.' This is why the first two-thirds of the twentieth century was dominated by what I have called 'the passion for the Real': what the nineteenth century dreamed of and experimented with, the twentieth century had to accomplish fully.[3]

This obsession with victory and the Real was focused on problems of organization and discipline, and entirely contained, from Lenin's *What Is to Be Done?* of 1902, in the theory and practice of the centralized and homogeneous class party. We can say that the communist parties embodied, in their 'iron discipline', the Real of the communist hypothesis.

This characteristic construction of the second sequence of the hypothesis, the party, in effect resolved the question bequeathed by the first sequence, and especially by the Paris Commune, which had been its apogee and its end: the question of victory. In Russia, China and Czechoslovakia, in Albania, Korea and Vietnam, even in Cuba if a bit differently, a complete revolution in the political and social order was accomplished under the leadership of communist parties, by insurrection or protracted people's war, and endured in the form of what has been called the 'socialist state'. After the first sequence, which went under the sign of the formulation of the communist hypothesis and its reality as

3 I have offered a detailed analysis of the 'passion for the Real' as a typical subjective form of the twentieth century in my book *The Century* (Cambridge: Polity, 2007).

a movement, there was then this second sequence, under the sign of its disciplined and militarized organization, its local victory and its duration.

As is only normal, the second sequence in its turn created a problem that it lacked the means to resolve, by the very methods that had enabled it to resolve the problem handed down by the first sequence. The party, in fact, appropriate for insurrectionary or military victory over weakened reactionary powers, proved ill-adapted for the construction of a state of proletarian dictatorship in Marx's sense, in other words a state organizing the transition towards a non-state, a power of non-power, a dialectical form of the withering away of the state. The form of the party-state, on the contrary, involved an experiment with an unprecedented form of authoritarian or even terroristic state, one that in any case was entirely separate from people's practical life. A number of achievements of these 'Socialist' states were remarkable, in such fields as education, public health, everyday ideology (the formal valorization of working people) and public order. On an international level, these states made their imperialist counterparts sufficiently afraid that the latter were compelled, externally as well as internally, to exercise a caution that we much regret today, when the arrogance of a capitalism that has reached its highest stage no longer knows any limits. And yet the state principle was inherently tainted and in the end ineffective. The deployment of extreme and bloody police violence was in no way sufficient to rescue it from its internal bureaucratic inertia and, in the ferocious competition imposed on it by its adversaries, it took scarcely more than fifty years to show that it would never carry the day.

It was the party's inadequacy when it came to ensuring

the real duration and creative transformation of the communist hypothesis that prompted the final major convulsions of the second sequence: the Cultural Revolution in China, and the nebulous event called 'May '68' in France. In China, Mao's maxim on this subject was 'No communism without a communist movement.' It was necessary, whatever the cost, to steep the party in the mass movement in order to regenerate it, to de-bureaucratize it, and launch it on the transformation of the real world. The Cultural Revolution attempted this test, and rapidly became chaotic and violent, given that the definition of the enemy was uncertain, and that it was directed against the single pillar of society: the Communist Party itself.[4] Mao is not blameless for this, as he declared, 'Don't you know where the bourgeoisie is? It's within the Communist Party!' Eventually, for want of support for the most radical experiments in the decentralization of the state (the 'Shanghai Commune' of early 1967), the old order had to be re-established in the worst conditions. In France, after May '68, the dominant theme was that organized collective action had to create new spaces of politics, and not reproduce the centralized management of the state.[5] The main content was new forms of organization and action that embraced intellectuals and workers in the same political vision, and proposed to make the communist hypothesis endure even

4 For an idea of what I think of the Chinese Cultural Revolution, and the use I have made of it, see the pamphlet *La Révolution Culturelle: la dernière révolution?*, published in the context of the Conférences du Rouge Gorge, which Natacha Michel and I established and led between 2001 and 2005. This can be obtained from *Le Journal Politique* (Chapter 3, Note 1). [See also *Polemics* (London: Verso 2006.)]

5 On May '68, taken in its genuine political essence and not as a cultural 'crisis' of youth, see the lecture by Natacha Michel *O Jeunesse! O Vieillesse!*, published in the context of the Conférences du Rouge Gorge. Natacha Michel, a major novelist, discovered the language in which to unfold this experience. Cf. *La Chine européenne* (Paris: Gallimard, 1975) and *Circulaire à toute ma via humaine* (Paris: Seuil, 2005).

outside the logic of the seizure of power. However, even if this experiment was continued in new forms, we can say that from the end of the 1970s and on a global scale the modern form of the reactionary state, capitalo-parliamentarism, regained its dominance over people's minds, under cover of 'democracy'. Let us say that the political processes of a new type arc at a similar stage to that occupied by Lenin at the very start of the twentieth century, when the question 'What is to be done?' could be given precise experimental answers, in a general context dominated by the adversary, and which slowly but surely advanced towards that acceleration of the subjective phenomena that war always proposes.[6]

Let us recall, in fact, that between the first and the second sequence, between late Marx and early Lenin, there were forty years of triumphant imperialism. The period from the repression of the Paris Commune to the First World War saw the apogee of the bourgeoisie, which occupied the whole planet, laying waste and pillaging whole continents. I am talking about sequences of the communist hypothesis, but

---

6 Among the long or short political sequences identified as working from the mid-1970s onwards to re-establish the communist hypothesis (even if the word itself was often shunned), in other words to transform, in opposition to the domination of capitalo-parliamentarism, the relationship between politics and the state, we can mention the following: the first two years of the Portuguese revolution; the very first sequence of the Solidarity movement in Poland, particularly in the factories; the first phase of the insurrection against the Shah in Iran; the creation of the Organisation Politique in France; and the Zapatista movement in Mexico. Today, we need to investigate the real nature of the link to the people, from the standpoint of the universal lessons to be drawn, of organizations limited by their religious allegiance: Hezbollah in Lebanon and Hamas in Palestine. We should also pay attention to the countless worker and peasant uprisings in China, and the actions of the 'Maoists' in India and Nepal. The list is by no means closed. [The Organisation Politique is the formation with which Badiou is associated in France and which is particularly invested in the struggles of undocumented foreign workers. For more on the OP and Badiou, see Peter Hallward's *Badiou: A Subject to Truth* (Minneapolis: The University of Minnesota Press, 2003) and the introduction and interview in Badiou's *Ethics* (London: Verso, 2002).]

these sequences are separated by intervals in which it is by no means the communist hypothesis that is dominant, in terms of equilibrium and stabilization. It is then declared on the contrary that this hypothesis is untenable, even absurd and criminal, and has to be abandoned. And so we are back with Sarkozy, seeking to put an end to May '68 once and for all.

This authorizes us to return to the question: Where are we now? Let us accept that on a world scale, the second sequence came to an end in the late 1970s. And that since then, drawing the lessons of the critical experiments that marked the final phase of this sequence, May '68 and the Cultural Revolution, various collectives have been seeking the path of a politics of emancipation that is adequate to the present time. We are then in the context of a new interval phase, a phase in which the adversary appears to be triumphant. We can, for example, describe what is happening in France without discouragement or concession: in other words, the reappearance of forms of the Pétainist transcendental embodied in the state. This is not an aberrant or discordant phenomenon that needs to depress us. It is a local crystallization of the fact that we find ourselves in an interval phase, such as previously existed, for a long while, in the late nineteenth and early twentieth centuries. Now we know that, in this kind of circumstance, what is on the agenda is the opening of a new sequence of the communist hypothesis. The only problem is that of the scope of the catastrophe that war, an inevitable convulsion of imperialism, will impose on humanity as the price of an advance, a step forward, of what alone will organize its salvation: communist egalitarianism, this time on a worldwide scale.

Those of us who remember May '68 and the Cultural

Revolution absolutely must transmit to the scattered militants of the communist hypothesis a rational certainty, already immanent at these intense political moments: what will come will not be, and cannot be, a continuation of the second sequence. Marxism, the workers' movement, mass democracy, Leninism, the proletarian party, the Socialist state – all these remarkable inventions of the twentieth century – are no longer of practical use. At the theoretical level, they certainly deserve further study and consideration; but at the level of politics, they have become impracticable. This is a first point of essential awareness: the second sequence is closed, and it is no good trying to continue or restore it.

The truth, which already began to make itself apparent in the 1960s, is that our problem is neither that of the popular movement as bearer of a new hypothesis, nor that of the proletarian party as victorious leader of the realization of this hypothesis. The strategic problem bound up with the third sequence, for the opening of which we are now working, is something else.

Since we are in an interval phase dominated by the enemy, and new experiments are still tightly circumscribed, I am not in a position to tell you with any certainty what will be the essence of the third period that is going to open up. The general direction, however, what we can call the abstract philosophy of the thing, seems clear to me: it involves a new relationship between the real political movement and ideology. This already underlay the expression 'cultural revolution', and Mao's dictum 'To have order in organization, it is necessary first to have order in ideology.' It is also what underlay the idea, common after May '68, of the 'revolutionizing of minds'.

The communist hypothesis as such is generic, it is the

basis of any emancipatory orientation, it names the sole thing that is worthwhile if we are interested in politics and history. But the way that the hypothesis presents itself determines a sequence: a new way for the hypothesis to be present in the interiority of new forms of organization and action.

It should be understood that in one form or another we shall retain the theoretical and historical teachings that issued from the first sequence and the central function of victorious discipline that issued from the second. And yet our problem today is neither the existence of the hypothesis as a movement, nor its disciplined victory at the level of the state. Our problem is the specific modality in which the thought prescribed by the hypothesis presents itself in the figures of action. In other words, a new relationship between the subjective and the objective, which is neither a multiform movement inspired by the intelligence of the multitude (as Negri and the alter-globalists believe), nor a renewed and democratized party (as the Trotskyists and ossified Maoists believe). The (workers') movement of the nineteenth century and the (Communist) party of the twentieth century were forms of material presentation of the communist hypothesis. It is impossible to return to either of these. What then could be the moving force of this presentation for the twenty-first century?

We should note that in the nineteenth century, the great question first of all was, quite simply, that of the *existence* of the communist hypothesis. When Marx said that the spectre of communism was haunting Europe, he meant: the hypothesis is here, we have established it. The second sequence, that of the revolutionary party with its iron discipline, the militarization of the class war, the Socialist state, was undoubtedly the sequence of a victorious representation of the hypothesis. Yet this representation preserved the characteristics of the first sequence, in particular the idea of overthrow ('the world will turn on its foundations'), the idea of the revolution as a global day of reckoning. We can say that victory was still conceived as the victory of *the first form of the hypothesis*.

The task facing us, after the negative experience of the socialist states, and the ambiguous lessons of the Cultural Revolution and May '68 – and this is why our research is so complicated, so erratic, so experimental – is to bring the communist hypothesis into existence in a different modality from that of the previous sequence. The communist hypothesis remains the right hypothesis, as I have said, and I do not see any other. If this hypothesis should have to be abandoned, then it is not worth doing anything in the order of collective action. Without the perspective of communism, without this Idea, nothing in the historical and political future is of such a kind as to interest the philosopher. Each individual can pursue their private business, and we won't mention it again. The Rat Man would then be right, as he is credited by some former communists, whether eager for positions or simply lacking any courage. But holding on to the Idea, the existence of the hypothesis, does not mean that its first form of presentation, focused on property and the state, must be maintained just as it is. In fact, what we are ascribed as a philosophical task, we could say even a duty, is to help a new modality of existence of the hypothesis to come into being. New in terms of the type of political experimentation to which this hypothesis could give rise. We have learned from the second sequence and its final efforts that we have to go back to the conditions of existence of the communist hypothesis, and not just perfect its means. We cannot rest content with the dialectical relationship between the state and the mass movement, the preparation for insurrection, and the construction of a powerful and disciplined organization. We must actually re-establish the hypothesis in the field of ideology and action.

To support the communist hypothesis today, in local experiments with politics, experiments that enable us to maintain, against the established domination of reaction, what I call a point, in other words a specific duration, a particular consistency: that is the minimum condition for the maintenance of the hypothesis to appear also as the transformation of its self-evidence.

In this respect, we are closer to a set of problems already examined in the nineteenth century than we are to the great history of the revolutions of the twentieth century. We are dealing, as in the 1840s, with absolutely cynical capitalists, ever more inspired by the idea that it is only wealth that counts, that the poor are simply lazy, that Africans are backward, and that the future, with no discernible limit, belongs to the 'civilized' bourgeoisies of the Western world. All kinds of phenomena from the nineteenth century are reappearing: extraordinarily widespread zones of poverty, within the rich countries as well as in the zones that are neglected or pillaged, inequalities that constantly grow, a radical divide between working people – or those without work – and the intermediate classes, the complete dissolution of political power into the service of wealth, the disorganization of the revolutionaries, the nihilistic despair of wide sections of young people, the servility of a large majority of intellectuals, the determined but very restricted experimental activity of a few groups seeking contemporary ways to express the communist hypothesis . . . Which is no doubt why, as also happened in the nineteenth century, it is not the victory of the hypothesis that is on the agenda today, as everyone knows, but its conditions of existence. And this was the great question of the revolutionaries of the nineteenth century: first of all, to make the hypothesis exist. Well, that is again our task, in the interval phase that we find so oppressive. But it is exalting: through a combination of constructions of thought, which are always global or universal, and political experiments, which are local or singular but can be transmitted universally, we can assure the new existence of the communist hypothesis, both in consciousness and in concrete situations.